WHAT PEOPLE AF
WINNING THE W

"If your organization wants to win the war for talent, then Kevin Stakelum's new book, *Winning the War for Talent,* is your battle guide! Kevin's background in talent acquisition serves the reader who is struggling with solving today's tough staffing issues. A must-read for every HR and organizational leader who wants to source the best talent."

—Cathy Fyock, Author, *The Truth About Hiring the Best*

"As head of a startup investigations company, I was struggling to know when and who to hire while simultaneously worrying about the costs of additional personnel. Working with Kevin, confidence in hiring was achieved and an immediate boost in company revenue occurred. The lessons in *Winning the War for Talent* are presented effectively through a commonsense approach which I believe every small company can benefit from. If you are curious how to grow your business through impactful hiring practices, this book is a must read and Kevin Stakelum is a definite resource for you and your team."

—David P. Jude, Managing Member / Chief Investigator, DPJ Consulting, LLC

"With competition for talent at an all-time high, *Winning the War for Talent* is a game-changer and must-read for anyone serious about winning. Most books I've read on the topic focus solely on the perceived problems, which left me wondering what to do next. Yet others jumped straight to solutions, which, without context, were often useless. This book, however, is different. I got a clear and insightful view into root causes of problems, practical solutions to address the problems, and even key metrics/data to consider. I call that winning!"

—John E. Brown, Jr., Chief People Officer, GEHA, Inc.

"Whether you're a new or a seasoned leader, this book provides clear and actionable tasks. It seems like we're always in a war for talent and this is a great playbook that everyone should have in their arsenal."

—Ben Martin, Director, Talent Acquisition, Promethean

Talent identification is a critical business imperative, particularly when there is a talent supply shortage, such as in the aftermath of COVID-19 or amidst continuing digital disruption across industries. In his book, *Winning the War for Talent*, Kevin Stakelum addresses many of the traditional talent acquisition strategies that are fundamental to the success of all types of organizations. What differentiates this book from others is the inclusion of data analysis in the acquisition process. The business processes and data gathering techniques included in the book give leaders at all levels the information they require to implement data-driven strategies that will help them to attract the talent they need to succeed!

—Gerald Kane, C. Herman and Mary Virginia Terry Chair in Business Administration, Terry College of Business, University of Georgia

WINNING
THE WAR FOR
TALENT

Talent Acquisition Strategies for Today's Business Leaders

KEVIN STAKELUM

Publishing support provided by
Ignite Press
5070 N. Sixth St. #189
Fresno, CA 93710
www.IgnitePress.us

ISBN: 979-8-9871644-0-2
ISBN: 979-8-9871644-1-9 (Ebook)

For bulk purchase and for booking, contact:

Kevin Stakelum
Kevin@stakelum.com
www.Stakelum.com

Library of Congress Control Number: 2022919435

Cover design by Jibin Joy
Edited by Charlie Wormhoudt
Interior design by Eswari Kamireddy

FIRST EDITION

This book is reflective of a lifetime commitment to the art and skill of talent acquisition. It is dedicated to my wife, my children, and all my close friends who encouraged me to engage in this adventure. It is also dedicated to countless co-workers and business partners who helped me to discover the challenges and design the solutions presented.

ACKNOWLEDGMENTS

I want to thank my editorial board, my coach, my editor, and all of the people who helped me to formulate the components of this book. Without them, this project would have never been completed.

CONTENTS

Introduction   xi

SECTION 1: BUSINESS AND OPERATIONS

CHAPTER 1: KEY BUSINESS PRINCIPLES OF THE
          RECRUITING PROCESS   3
CHAPTER 2: CONSUMERIZATION OF TALENT ACQUISITION   7
CHAPTER 3: MANAGING THE TALENT ACQUISITION PROCESS
          USING AUTOMATION   15
CHAPTER 4: TALENT ACQUISITION VS. FILLING
          REQUISITIONS   23
CHAPTER 5: DIVERSITY RECRUITING   27
CHAPTER 6: RESOURCING YOUR RECRUITING TEAMS
          EFFICIENTLY THROUGH FLEXIBLE EMPLOYMENT 33
CHAPTER 7: HOW DOES YOUR PROCESS RUN?   41

SECTION 2: PROCESS EXECUTION

CHAPTER 8: REQUISITION PREPARATION   47
CHAPTER 9: GO TO MARKET   59
CHAPTER 10: THE SEARCH IS ON!   71
CHAPTER 11: ASSESSING TALENT   85
CHAPTER 12: CHOOSING THE BEST CANDIDATE AND
          CLOSING THEM   97
CHAPTER 13: LAUNCHING THEIR CAREER WITH YOU   105

Conclusion   117
About the Author   123

INTRODUCTION

You often hear about the "war for talent." I see evidence of it often and I understand the reality of it. If your team has experience with the complications caused by a difficulty in quickly finding the right talent, this book is for you!

I was meeting with colleagues not long ago for lunch. As I sat down, I overheard a part of a conversation between Jan and Bill:

Bill: "...the thing that keeps me awake at night is the lack of talent that is available for my team to complete the work assigned to us."

Jan: "I agree, we seem to get many resumes, but the resumes do not fit what we are looking for in the position. It takes too long to fill the role and by the time I do, someone else has resigned and we are right back to where we were when we started. Isn't there a better way to find the best talent that we need?"

These are some of the challenges I will cover in this book. I have separated the book into two sections. The first deals with recruiting as a business function and the second studies the challenges and suggested solutions for the interview process.

Here is a brief preview of what you will find in the sections and chapters ahead.

Section 1: Business and Operations – Discusses the recruiting landscape and some of the aspects of acquisition as a business process.

Chapter 1: Key Business Principles of the Recruiting Process – Your interviewing process should be business focused, candidate focused, and rely heavily on the partnership between the teams involved in the recruiting process.

Chapter 2: Consumerization of Talent Acquisition – Candidates are more like consumers of your company's hiring processes than ever before. Are you creating the same type of process for them that you do for customers? The rise in visibility of processes, status, and satisfaction ratings are changing. Have your recruiting processes done the same?

Chapter 3: Managing Talent Acquisition Processes using Automation – Process automation allows for consistency and quality control of the information being shared. Are your teams using the data generated to improve the hiring results?

Chapter 4: Talent Acquisition vs. Filling Requisitions – Hiring teams often get too focused on pedigree and checklists instead of finding the talent needed to complete the duties of the currently open positions. Are your teams more focused on hitting a number and checking boxes than adding great talent to the company?

Chapter 5: Diversity Recruiting – Diversity Recruiting goes way beyond ethnicity and gender. Are your teams maximizing the unemployed and underemployed populations who may not respond to traditional mass market advertising? Veterans and their spouses, entry level, retiree, and disability hiring initiatives are all ways to increase the candidate pool while strengthening the diversity of your team and company.

Chapter 6: Resourcing your Recruiting Teams – Your recruiting team is a production-based department. The switch from thinking about the "number of recruiters" to utilizing a "resource model" can help to control costs and provide flexibility to your recruiting team needs. It also allows you to align special projects more closely to the recruiting costs associated with staffing them. Are you also including internal resources to improve the business results of your recruiting efforts?

Chapter 7: How Does Your Process Run? – Have you ever tried applying to your own jobs? Is it easy? Does the candidate experience match the experience you want to provide to your customers?

Section 2: Process Execution – We will look at the six steps of the interview process I have identified and assess how you feel each is performing for you.

Chapter 8: Requisition Preparation – How well are your teams preparing for the interview process and how are they doing even when there are no open requisitions? Does everyone know their role and agree on the desired priorities and outcomes?

Chapter 9: Go to Market – Are your interview teams ready to respond to applicants quickly and consistently? What are the practices you want to encourage in considering internal and external candidates?

Chapter 10: The Search is On! – In a labor shortage, speed of response and consistency of communication are very important. Does the way you treat the large number of people who apply but do not get the job align to how you want to treat your customers?

Chapter 11: Assessing Talent – Do different processes for the same position yield different results? How are you ensuring the hiring team knows what it takes to be successful and can identify it in others?

Chapter 12: Choosing the Best Candidate – Do you maximize the effectiveness and minimize the cost to the organization? We will discuss ways to optimize both.

Chapter 13: Launching their career with you – Does your team differentiate between onboarding and orientation? What is the difference, and why is it so important to do both well?

Concluding thoughts – Putting all the pieces together. You will do well in some areas and need to improve in others. Using cost and experience to prioritize the work, this book gives you solutions which will improve the portions of the process most important to you. It also assists you by providing links for additional content and information to help you. The key to winning the war on talent is to recognize recruiting as a business function and to make the process include a focus on generating a positive candidate experience.

In my experience implementing the changes presented in this book, the impact has been significant, regardless of the size of the organization. The process changes have returned as much as 60% of the investment required. I have increased acquisition and interview capacity to improve the support for changing hiring needs and have documented them to be consistently applied across organizations. There has been as much as a 10% decrease in attrition through using some of the internal mobility concepts.

At the end of every chapter, there will be an opportunity to reflect on your experiences, encourage self-assessments, and obtain additional information regarding how the contents apply to your business.

As you read the book, I expect some ideas will be more interesting than others, and some will be like what you are already doing. There will also be some activities which have different components, depending on which level within your organization you are assessing. For example, the high-volume call center positions may have more opportunity to be more efficient than those of your corporate functions. The questions at the end of each chapter will help you to identify which of the recommendations will have the largest impact in each of those departments.

SECTION 1:
BUSINESS AND OPERATIONS

Before we look at the steps of the recruiting process, we will look at establishing some metrics and tools of the talent acquisition function that are used to create a starting point for the rest of the book.

1

KEY BUSINESS PRINCIPLES OF THE RECRUITING PROCESS

Many business leaders think of recruiting as an administrative function and that is what Bill and Jan were doing when we met them in the introduction. A common sentiment is, "We need more resumes to find the very best." Instead, recruiting should be considered a business function which adds a great deal of value to the financial and performance capability within an organization. Due to the high volume of activity the hiring process represents, it is important to treat it like an outreach function with a set goal (find the best talent available) while also introducing your company to prospective customers. The application process can be used to capture a great amount of data. When companies capture it and utilize it effectively, it may yield fewer candidates at first, but these candidates will already be pre-qualified.

Over time, hit rates and efficiency measures (presented in Chapter 3) will reflect the improved quality of the candidates you are interested in. The candidates represent a population of people who are interested in working for your company, so cultivating interest saves time and money.

Application data can be used to target the specific people you want to speak to for other positions as well. Those candidates can then be invited to apply to other positions they may be interested in and had not considered. In addition to providing more information about the company, this will also change the relationship from a negative one to one holding promise. The impact of being rejected from one position changes from a process that ends to a process that begins and is continued as new roles become available. Good companies focus on this continuation and recognize the candidate pool has changed. It is not enough to just consider candidates for the role they apply for. Providing them the service of routing them to other positions shows you value them while giving your hiring teams a quick pool of candidates who have met some criteria for their current and future openings.

Additionally, efficiencies gained by reducing such high-volume processes will combine to represent significant savings. These savings come in the form of marketing and travel expenses, interview time, and the time it takes interview teams to speak to all who responded. Hiring teams usually do a great job of treating the candidates they hire well. The rest of this population often walks away with a negative view of the company.

Using Metrics

Using data and metrics, the talent acquisition (TA) team can play a pivotal role in focusing on those business problems which will have the biggest impact.

Successfully identifying and using relevant metrics provides your company with a huge competitive advantage over those companies that do not. Some of the improvements are performance based but some activities can be directly impacted and measured.

Every company must deal with hiring as a major financial planning point regardless of the size of the company. In most companies it represents one of the top three expense categories. When leaders think of recruiting, they often think of it as being overhead with little business advantage other than completing the administrative tasks of moving candidates quickly through a process. Using data to act more strategically and provide more value to the candidate will help you to build a stronger product brand by creating a recruiting brand. Many current processes have been modified to allow the ease of application. If that is not paired with a restructuring of the rest of the process, then companies are just spending time and money generating more potential customers who are unsatisfied with the outcome.

Getting the Most out of Your Career Advertising Activities

Many leaders find it remarkable and surprising to learn 50–75% of a company's hiring comes in the form of replacement hiring. At that rate, you are basically replacing the workforce an approximate average of every two years. This attrition rate costs money and addressing it can be a key source of savings. Obviously, the company rate is going to be driven more by some departments than others. Often it occurs in the lower-level positions and in the organizations that are completing most of the hiring. A portion of replacement hiring (attrition) is "good," meaning that the employee was ready to move on or was made qualified for higher roles in other companies. Usually it only accounts for about 10% of the current population. The rest has resulted in wasted effort and damages the organization's hiring brand. The best organizations have realized the best way to fund innovations, improve results, and reduce recruiting and interviewing costs is to improve the hit rate. The hit rate is expressed as a percentage and is defined as the number of offers accepted in relation to the total number of interviews. This can be measured using the following cost per hire ratio:

Number of candidates interviewed / Offers accepted

When designing the interviewing process use the following guiding principles:

- Business focused with measurable financial implications
- Candidate focused with the understanding that candidates are future potential customers
- Designed as a partnership with all involved to identify and address challenges with the process as they occur

Companies doing this well will hold a competitive advantage in terms of a lower time to fill, a lower cost of the process, and the ability to apply these efficiencies to positively impact a broader set of candidates.

THINGS TO CONSIDER:

Have you ever looked at the candidate generation results for your organization? Specifically look at the following:

- **Time to fill** – How long does it take from deciding to open a position to getting an acceptance?
- **Touch percentage** – What percent of candidates that apply get looked at and assessed?
- What is the **interview to offer ratio** for your team? If you could get the same number of hires, of the same quality of candidates, and do it using half of the interview time (thus saving productivity, financial, and bandwidth expenses), how might you do that?
- What is the **hit rate** for your organization and for each department that is hiring? What financial benefits could a better hit rate and attrition rate reasonably provide to your organization?

Set up the processes discussed for a few key positions within your team and see what you discover. We will also discuss this in more detail throughout the book.
Go to https://winningthewarfortalent.org for more information.

2

CONSUMERIZATION OF TALENT ACQUISITION

I was attending a meeting a few weeks ago. As we were waiting for the meeting to start, I asked two of the people present who I knew were looking for a new position (I will refer to them as Miguel and Sue) a simple question: "How is your job search going?"

Sue: "It is not going well. I have literally applied for a hundred roles that I meet the stated requirements for, and it is like sending my resume into a black hole. I never hear back from the company, or I receive a computerized form letter "regretting to inform you that we have decided to choose someone else." Some even apologize for me being unqualified for the role, although I have performed the same job at an elevated level for five years and meet ALL their qualifications."

Miguel: "Yes, the other day, I received a rejection letter from a position that I applied for nine months ago. By that time, I could barely remember which position they were referring to. Why did it take nine months to determine my qualifications?"

Sue: "Yes. I can order almost anything to be delivered to my home. I can check on the status of the order, and I am notified at each step where they are in fulfilling my order. Why can't companies do that for me as a candidate?"

Miguel: "It makes me wonder if they even looked at my

resume. Based upon how they treated me as a candidate, I have stopped buying their product. I don't want to support a company that treats prospective employees this way."

A great deal of activity goes into the identification, targeted outreach, and assessment of candidates. Unlike other outreach functions for your team, only 2–5% of those who respond will reach what they see as a favorable outcome. The handling of the other 95–98% is especially important. There are very few business functions which would focus primarily on those who had a successful result and ignore the experience of the other 95–98% of potential customers. Several studies confirm how a candidate is treated in the application process reflects how they view your company's products.

Candidates are more like consumers of your company's hiring processes than ever before. Are you creating the same type of process for them as you do for customers? The rise in visibility of processes, status, and satisfaction ratings are changing, have your recruiting processes done the same?

With the introduction of flexibility and transparency in the delivery of products and services, there has been a shift in the expectations of candidates. Your candidates live in a world where a consumer can compare prices for products and services. They can order at any time, check status, find their own consumer history, and access the information they see as being important whenever they want to. They can see contact information and the name of the person working on their order and know what kind of vehicle to expect it delivered in. Candidates are now asking why they cannot get similar service in the interview process. With the extended reach companies now have with applicants, shortcomings become magnified. We can illustrate this using a funnel report.

The Funnel

One useful data set can be generated by creating a funnel report which can be replicated at several levels within the company. The chart below is for each position open. Some profiles will attract more candidates, and some will attract fewer, but this is a good average volume to demonstrate what I am talking about in this chapter.

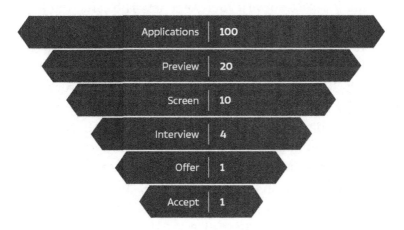

For the one open position to be filled, there are 100 candidates:

- 80, who are interested in the role and your company, will not be seen or considered
- 20 will be looked at in consideration for your role
- 10 will be screened
- 4 candidates considered qualified will be interviewed
- 1 offer will be extended and accepted

In this example, of the 100 applicants only 20 are going to be reviewed simply because the review process is manual and

recruiting departments are usually resourced based upon number of hires to be made instead of by how many candidates they
review. For some companies, there is no attempt to preview all
the candidates, so the interview teams spend their time talking
to candidates who are not qualified. As a result, 80% of the total applicants are not being considered, even if they are qualified
for the role they applied for. In most companies and departments,
they will not be contacted for any other role they may be a fit
for. This figure of 80% represents sunk cost and opportunity lost.
Your team has paid to reach out to them, and you will receive no
value from the communication. They will be provided with no value in their interaction with your company. The candidates want to
work for you. They have taken the time to engage your company
and have responded to the "call to action" by submitting their resume. They feel they match the criteria you have indicated you
need. This 80% will have no interaction with your company, other
than a rejection email. This experience will damage your product
brand, your company brand, and your hiring brand, and will do so
for very large numbers of applicants. In most models, unless they
apply for another role, they will not be considered for other roles
with your company. In a talent shortage, the likelihood of them
applying to other positions now or in the future is small. It is easier
for them to apply somewhere else and there are plenty of options
to choose from. This represents a significant opportunity lost in
terms of their candidacy and their opinion of you as a business
partner. We refer to this as "poisoning the pool." Your company
would have been better off not advertising to them, and they are
not likely to be interested in your future positions.

An Alternative:

If you look at it as a data gathering exercise, you can be accumu-
lating an enormously powerful data set which can be used to fill
current and future positions. Your team will also be making these
candidates feel better more quickly about the relationship you

are building with them. You will be able to update them at each step, and at each step you can provide information educating them about your company.

Examples:

Finding ways to engage the majority and to use their interest to improve future business results is important and the figures outlined above clearly represent why. The cost of interest generation has been incurred so it is important to think of ways to maximize its impact. For example, instead of asking if they are available to work 9 am to 5 pm, other questions could be seamlessly inserted.

"Our company works in three shifts:

- 8 am–4 pm – First Shift
- 4 pm–Midnight – Second Shift
- Midnight–8 pm – Third Shift

"Our pay for all shifts is competitive and there is a $1 shift differential for the second shift and a $2 shift differential for the third shift. The current opening is for the first shift but please check on every shift you may be interested in being contacted for."

The best organizations now capture the data. When future positions become open for second and third shifts, there is a list of people who have indicated they are interested in being considered for those shifts. Those organizations save time and money in contacting interested candidates instead of only capturing those who actively apply. The organization is also providing a service to candidates by inviting them to apply to new openings they may not be aware of. In this way, relationships are formed, and those relationships add value to the organization and its hiring brand.

Another example could be for a position that requires language skills. Instead of asking them if they are fluent in Spanish, the question could be something like, "Please check all the languages you are considered fluent in."

The same logic applies to positions like physicians, nurses, truck drivers, and others.

In the example above, the beginning of the process can be automated to handle the volume, and then the candidate can be quickly contacted in person to build a relationship with them. Automation can also be used to maximize consistency of message and to quickly identify where the candidate stands in the process. This process can apply to all applicants so 100% of those who engage get a quick response and interaction in a way that shows a person is reviewing their information.

This would be accomplished by using what we call "knock-in questions." Many of the most successful recruiting teams are using this process to strengthen their candidate pool now and in the future. Information would be provided about your company, your team, and your opportunity. Information would be gathered about their interests, availability, and experiences. It would always be available for candidates to learn about your team, and it would be curated and managed in bulk through the recruiting team. The candidate/potential customer now can check their status in the process. The process becomes more of a series of relationship building exercises than just an administrative task. Since it is automated, it is not dependent on individual recruiters. If a recruiter moves due to a changing priority of positions, the service and experience of the current candidates would not change. Here is how it may look:

Changing the Funnel

In order to maximize the impact that advertising and responses have on your recruiting efforts, there should be a change in the funnel. Every candidate who applies should be considered using technology and qualifications stated in the job descriptions.

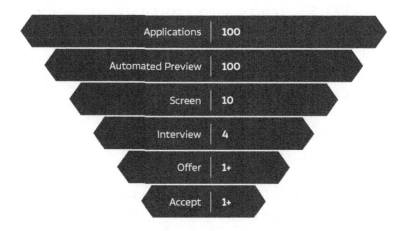

- 100 people apply
- 100 people are previewed by a person using automation and a series of knock-in questions
- Technology captures the data to help determine the best ten to screen
- Four are interviewed
- All who are qualified are offered
- All who applied can now be considered for other positions which require the skills they possess. This can be done in a clear, consistent, and measurable way which adds value to the candidate and the company. The volume of applicants for high-volume jobs can be used to also fill lower-volume, similar jobs.

In the next chapter, we will go into detail regarding how this works with automation, but this is the experience great hiring teams are trying to create.

THINGS TO CONSIDER:

- Is your team generating any type of funnel analysis? If so, what have you noticed and how have you acted upon it? If not, why not?
- How interactive is your process? Does the candidate get value from applying to your positions? What is it they gain?

Feel free to share your answers at
https://winningthewarfortalent.org.

3

MANAGING THE TALENT ACQUISITION PROCESS USING AUTOMATION

When I mention the topic of automation in the interview process to my classes at the University of Louisville, the feeling is negative. One student shared, "I would rather speak to a real person instead of just speaking to a computer." When I altered the scenario to include the process discussed in Chapter 2, their answers changed. They would prefer to have information available to them if it gives them the same chance to apply as everyone else. It was then I realized the best way to introduce technology into the talent war is to start with a focus on them as a candidate.

Instead of only thinking of using the technology to improve production and reduce costs (which it can), great companies present it as a way to improve the service to the applicants. Electronic interviews (recorded video, recorded audio, live video, texts) can be seen as impersonal methods focussed on improving the efficiency of the company. It could also be a tool allowing candidates to thoughtfully complete their first few rounds of interviews at a time best for them. Instead of having to wait weeks to speak to a recruiter from 8 am to 5 pm in the recruiter's time zone, they can complete the interview as quickly as they want. The application can be customized by them to fit their schedule. Instead of the few candidates who get a response having to go through a couple of basic screening calls, everyone answers the key strategic questions which allow them to be considered for the current roles and for other roles in a consistent and measurable way. Their answers can then be used in a measurable way allowing them to be compared to others who are interested. With a time investment of approximately 60 minutes total, an applicant could apply, answer follow-on questions, and then schedule interviews for themselves. Candidates could easily access information, videos, and press releases giving them a better feel for the company and the work environment. There could be chatbots set up to answer a variety of questions in real time. A potential candidate could ask and answer questions prior to investing time to speak about opportunities within your company.

Automation

Many companies currently have moved to equating automation to easier applications for positions. If no other process is automated, the efforts to automate only benefit the company and provide no value to the candidate or to their experience. It also may not yield the best candidates. For automation to provide maximum value to the candidate, any time spent on their part should be spent in quick bursts or "micro-touches." It is an automated process but not an automatic one. The next step is human launched with automated results utilized by humans to make decisions. It also allows for human interventions if there is a question regarding the results. If done correctly, the administrative process of applicants applying for a job and never being contacted becomes a data analytics process allowing the company to better identify the candidate for other current openings. Their information can also be used to provide targeted qualification lists for positions they may be a good fit for at another date. It turns the relationship into one providing value, and the automation gives the recruiters the time to accomplish this task at scale. It also benefits candidates who complain about waiting for the recruiter to fit them into their schedule. Automation allows candidates to complete the process at their leisure and is not dependent on a certain time zone.

Using "Knock-In" vs. "Knock-Out" (KIKO) Questions in the Process

It is important to note that candidates should only be considered for positions they apply for and compared with other candidates using the same criteria. Automation just allows a company to benefit from the plethora of resumes and candidate information in the system to create "warm lists" of candidates who can be invited to consider and apply for all current and future openings. It changes the interaction from an administrative one ("Sorry you are not a good match for this role, check again later.") to a data analytics one focused on the candidate, such as: "Based upon information you previously supplied to us, we encourage you to look at this other position and apply to it if you are interested." The use of the KIKO concept changes the type of questions being asked. For example, instead of asking if they are a registered nurse, ask, "What is the highest form of nursing education you have completed?" In the first example, you are looking for a "knock-out" question specific to a position. In the second, you are instead using "knock-in" questions to help candidates to be notified of current or future openings they may not have otherwise been aware of. Your team has just provided a service to the candidate while lowering future advertising. It is scalable, reduces time to fill, and provides a service to the customer (the candidate) which transforms it into a business process.

Flexibility of Scheduling

The automation process provides a benefit to the candidate. Candidates can easily rely on the technology to complete the beginning steps with less of a time commitment. Applicants can focus on the presentation of their skills, and the automated system is available at all times in any time zone, independent of anyone else's availability. In less than one hour, the automation process described here identifies candidates within their schedule and informs them of a decision to proceed to team interviews. Using automation to present information and ask questions while being able to quickly answer them provides excellent value to the candidates. It also reduces time spent on leaving messages and coordinating conversations that ask the same questions automation can.

Flexibility of Scale

Technology can also be more effectively used in making interview processes possible in changing environments, allowing the recruiters to spend more time with candidates who are best suited for future discussions. It also allows for flexibility of scale. If demand increases, the screening portion of the interview process can expand. If hiring slows down, it can contract and recruiters and hiring teams would have bandwidth to start preparing for the next round of hiring. The recruiter and hiring team will then be able to spend more time in person with candidates who pass the first few automated steps. The amount of time an interview team spends does not change. The biggest difference automation allows is a higher percentage of interview time is spent on candidates who leaders know are better vetted. This improves the results of the process by getting more traction with candidates who are talented and can add value to your team.

Status Tracking and the Consumerization of Recruiting

Candidates are consumers of your interviewing practices, as are managers and other key stakeholders. With the introduction of status tracking for most delivered packages, the expectation in hiring is that the same experience should be provided. If it is not, then your organization is going to spend time updating and communicating manually. The automation of providing information will reduce time spent on answering questions, allowing the interview teams to spend their time more productively.

Virtual Job Simulations

> **The automation of providing information will reduce time spent on answering questions, allowing the interview teams to spend their time more productively.**

One capability electronic interviewing can incorporate into the screening process is a Virtual Job Simulation. Virtual Job Simulations are used to simulate the daily activities of the positions they represent. During one of my assignments, we were experiencing high turnover of candidates within a high-volume team. No matter how much we explained the role and the daily activities, candidates were still failing in their role within six months of being hired. Many were complaining about feeling like they were not prepared for the role despite undergoing six weeks of training. Using questions, video simulations, and assessment activities, top companies are providing the candidates with the opportunity to accurately simulate the experience of performing the tasks of the position. The simulations allowed candidates to compare their skills and abilities to those of top performers. They could complete the simulation on their schedule, and their screens were not based upon credentials, but were based on skill set. The simulations allowed them the option to remove themselves from the process if it was something they did not want to do. The initial screen and the Virtual Job Simulations were automated so recruiters spent less time on those candidates who were unqualified or uninterested in the positions available.

Three Tips for Designing Automation into the Interview Process

1. **Recognize all candidate groups are not the same**. The approach for specialized positions will look different than for more general positions. The best companies cater the tools to the candidate population. Keeping process design candidate focused allows your company to do both.
2. **Keep it simple and execute it well.** When done correctly the automated process can cut costs and be more efficient. Some of the savings will have to be reinvested into ongoing maintenance and design. Rolling out automation in small groups can be used to evaluate challenges, create best practices, and expand where necessary.
3. **See what your current vendors have available and see if you can maximize their features instead of adding additional independent systems.** The companies doing this best look first at the tools they currently have licenses for. Many provide additional services and product lines which can be utilized to create and enhance the streamlined processes discussed here. The tools are often easier to maintain, and the vendor is motivated to negotiate since you already have a relationship with them. Most will work with you to customize their tool to best fit your needs.

The recruiting business process does not have to be a restrictive set of rules which must be universally adhered to by all departments. There are certainly legal requirements governing the process and they are universal, but there is also a great deal of flexibility in how the process is driven. While the interviewing process is regulated, in the war for talent, it is a business process focused on producing a positive business outcome. Hiring in a high-volume scenario is going to require a different approach than a scenario hiring a few highly specialized employees.

THINGS TO CONSIDER:

- How automated is your recruiting process?
- The labor market has moved from a talent surplus to a war for talent. What is your company doing differently to attract talent?
- What service, information, or company knowledge do you share with your candidates? How are you ensuring consistency of message?

If you want to discuss this topic or if you need help designing your process, go to https://winningthewarfortalent.org.

4

TALENT ACQUISITION VS. FILLING REQUISITIONS

I was in an executive planning meeting with a growing company. They were going through some changes, and they mentioned that the finance team hiring was a key to their growth. They did not have enough people to complete assigned tasks quickly. As a result, they were using their senior team members to fill out basic reports. The CFO addressed the group and said, "Finding senior finance talent is the key to all of this. We can increase sales and service but if we do not modernize our financial processes, we will fail. We cannot get enough finance talent."

I was alarmed, so I approached the hiring manager to get his feedback regarding coverage for a currently open position. "I feel good about the current candidate pool. We have been speaking to candidates for six weeks now and we will decide over the next two weeks. We have four great candidates, all of whom would be a great addition to the team. We will pick one and then we will be done."

Later in the day, I spoke to the VP again and asked: "We have four great candidates—if this is so important, why is your team waiting for two more weeks and only trying to hire one? There is only one requisition, but shouldn't we offer them all? We would not only be adding to your team, but it would allow you to give your top performers a chance to do more meaningful work." He agreed. We made four offers; two joined the team and two had decided the process was taking too long and accepted an offer from another company.

Headcount Attainment

At any given moment, most companies are operating with approximately 93% of their planned headcount. This number is not always available to the hiring manager, but someone in the organization can decide to temporarily pre-hire for key departments. There are common reasons for considering this option:

1. Expected turnover – This may be due to normal turnover, but other factors impact this. The post-pandemic desire to work from home and the trend of early retirement come into play. Layoff concerns may increase attrition, even by those not affected.
2. Internal transfers – Key people moving into bigger roles or filling other needs in the company.
3. Expected growth – What is the budgetary growth in the department and what is the timing of it?
4. Targets of opportunity – You find a candidate with exceptional talent but have no currently vacant position.

In any case, pre-hiring for key positions is one way to win the war for talent. When you hire the candidates before you need them, you are giving them the opportunity to contribute and train before the urgency hits. You will be making them feel great about your faith in them. Hopefully, you are removing them from the available candidate pool of your competitors.

The automation mentioned in Chapter 3 identifies candidates in a consistent way. The ability to hire to respond to opportunities helps you to capitalize on the talent you have found. Flexibility in the timing of the hire helps you to win the war for talent.

THINGS TO CONSIDER:

- Do you have a process for granting pre-hire approval within your company? Do your leaders know about it?
- How do you plan to get ahead of headcount needs in a fiscally responsible way during a war for talent?

If you want to discuss this topic or if you need help designing your process, go to https://winningthewarfortalent.org.

5
DIVERSITY RECRUITING

External Recruiting

In meetings with managers about diversity recruiting I have often heard comments such as, "I don't care about the color of a person's skin, their religious beliefs, their age, or their gender affiliation. Find a qualified candidate for the role, and I will hire them." Or, "Capturing this information sounds like you want me to hire to a quota number and I will not do it."

There are four big reasons to automate as much of the process as possible:

1. **Capture data** – Are you successfully attracting a diverse candidate pool? Do the percentage of minorities who submit their applications match the minority percentage of the general population and of the population within your company?
2. **Reducing bias in the screening process** – There is an inherent bias in many facets of society. You will never eliminate it, but you can reduce it in the interview process by using the data to highlight anomalies in the performance of the process. Data-driven solutions shift the assessment

of skills to an equally comparable format, allowing decisions to be made based on data instead of bias. It is not foolproof and has to be monitored using the steps provided in this book, but automation quickly and easily gathers it into a format that can be operationalized.

3. **Providing opportunity –** The automation of the screening process is not an automatic solution. It will simply allow a company to determine the effectiveness of their process in fairly assessing candidates while adding value to the candidates. It is about providing the opportunity for all qualified candidates to be assessed consistently based solely on the skills needed to succeed in your company, regardless of current title, education level, or personal situation.

> **If your qualifiers are linked to other organizations instead of skill-based qualifications, then your attempt to broaden the candidate pool will be dependent on their candidate pools.**

4. **Remove artificial qualifiers –** Education level, previous experience in top Fortune 500 companies, and degrees from certain universities are not good indicators of whether someone is a good candidate. If your qualifiers are linked to other organizations instead of skill-based qualifications, then your attempt to broaden the candidate pool will be dependent on their candidate pools.

Today, so much emphasis is put upon resumes and social media presence and is not based upon whether the person can really do the job. The best organizations use the hiring process to present opportunity in a fair way and then reduce bias at each step of the process. The final decisions are based upon personal assessments and therefore open to bias, but it can be reduced by using data and monitoring the process at each step of the way. To be clear, this is not about lowering standards or hitting quotas. In a war for talent, organizations must spend time using mass marketing but must also focus on historically under-served populations. There are millions of candidates who fit into this category, so becoming good at diversity hiring is not about executing an administrative process. With the data, the recruiting efforts become a strategic business process designed specifically to help the business meet their hiring goals.

Focusing on all different types of diversity opens the opportunity to those populations and helps businesses to gain new areas of influence while attracting a broader array of talent. The decision to interview is based upon consistent and measurable criteria and can be analyzed and scientifically validated to identify anomalies in the system. Because this process directly relates to the topic of automation mentioned in the previous chapter, your company can achieve better results at a lower total operating cost than it does if you do nothing differently.

Internal Mobility

I have been involved in several projects where our increase in high-volume hiring caused a negative experience when minority candidates did not see a path to promotion equal to majority populations. It is easier to impact hiring numbers when there is a high volume of non-specialized positions. If you are successful in hiring minorities into lower-level positions, you must also ensure they are progressing within the company. It is much more difficult to effectively create opportunities to develop and advance those hires to impact the rest of the company starting from more specialized positions. Maximizing volume hiring to generate talent for the whole company is an area the best companies put their energy into. They view the hire as the beginning of a career journey and work to take advantage of the impact that candidates who join the organization in this way can have in other departments.

An alternative is to hire minority candidates directly into leadership roles. The challenge is that, systemically, there is a relatively small number of those candidates who have been given the opportunity to gain experience in higher positions. As a result, your company will have to be overly aggressive in attracting and compensating them and competition for those candidates will be very high. Without support, candidates who become leaders will become disenfranchised and will leave to explore the many other options they have. If they are properly supported, they will be able to thrive. They will also be in positions to help others to thrive as well.

Targeted Talent Pools

Like other candidate pools, each part of this population may need to be approached differently. They will have different expectations and needs, but here are some of the common communities your company should consider targeting:

- Veterans and spouses
- High school internships
- College internships
- People with disabilities
- Retirees or the soon to be retired
- Under-represented minorities
- College students with extended debt
- Minority professional organization members
- Students and alumni from Historically Black Colleges and Universities

In most cases, each population lends itself to distinct functions within your company, so creating a comprehensive program incorporating each of them is an effective way to attract them. The organizations which represent these groups provide helpful resources for creating hiring programs and consulting about challenges and issues as they arise. The organizations supporting each category offer training, employee and manager consulting, and funding to help to service their populations. Your company's efforts to support these under-utilized populations energizes the members of each, but also energizes anyone in your company who believes in any of these causes. The focus on these populations helps you to compete for new talent. In a labor surplus, they may be nice gestures your company can feel good about. In a war for talent, they are necessary to compete and win.

THINGS TO CONSIDER:

- Does your company monitor your minority hiring? How often, and at what level in the organization?
- Are there attraction and development plans to meet the needs of different populations?
- Rate your company's effectiveness in attracting and keeping candidates in the following populations, with ten being the highest and one being the lowest:
  o Veterans and their spouses
  o High school internships
  o College internships
  o People with disabilities
  o Retirees or the soon to be retired
  o Under-represented minorities
  o College students with extended debt
  o Minority professional organization members
  o HBCU students and alumni
- Have your leaders do the same and compare answers. What did you find?
- What efforts are you making towards maximizing the identification of great talent within these populations?

If you want to discuss this topic or see how others are doing this, go to https://winningthewarfortalent.org.

6

RESOURCING YOUR RECRUITING TEAMS EFFICIENTLY THROUGH FLEXIBLE EMPLOYMENT

I was speaking to a good friend of mine who is a talent acquisition leader. He had just taken a new position as a talent acquisition director, so I asked him how the new job was going. "I am very excited. I have my TA team and organization structure in place, we have clear goals and reporting, and we are ready to support the business most effectively. In fact, I was able to get a 'seat at the table' for my first executive leadership meeting last week!"

"That is great, how did the meeting go?" I asked.

"It was highly informative. We have some major growth and acquisitions coming up and each department head spoke about the resources they would need to support the growth. IT presented on hardware- and software-license resources it would need to add. Space planning, training, HR, all discussed their resource needs. As the meeting was adjourning, I asked about additional resourcing for the recruiting team."

Now I was curious: "So how did it go?"

He chuckled and then said, "Well at first there was a period of stunned silence. It seemed like no one had ever heard of resourcing the team that would have to hire the growing number of employees and all the support staff just discussed. The IT leader then scoffed and said, 'You have all the staff you need, just add this to their work. This is not much work when you divide it by all the recruiters.' I then attempted another approach: 'Our resources are fixed and produce a fixed number of hires per year. So, whose requisitions am I going to stop working on to shift my resources to staff this project?'"

Recruiting as an administrative function would just absorb the work, cut corners to complete the work, and sacrifice some quality to meet the unexpected demands. Recruiting as a business function looks at the situation with the same level of planning estimations and accountability other functions do.

Recruiting as an administrative function would just absorb the work, cut corners to complete the work, and sacrifice some quality to meet the unexpected demands. Recruiting as a business function looks at the situation with the same level of planning estimations and accountability other functions do. One thing I want to point out is the use of the word "resourcing" instead of "hiring recruiters."

Resourcing Options

So how do you apply options to your recruiting organization? Some types of resourcing are listed below with the strengths and weaknesses listed for each:

- **Full time exempt (FTE)** – This type of employee often shows up as headcount within a company and is regulated, usually by finance. They are costly in the sense that they require benefits and there is little flexibility to them. You can always offer them severance and downsize, but those are costly. Your company needs a number of FTEs to provide stability over time and to maximize the intellectual capital they will add to your function. They form the base of your company's recruiting team and can "flow to the work" as demand shifts.

- **Variable staffing pool (VSP)** – This pool can be used to fill cyclical hiring projects, and then they can be released until they are needed again. This type of employee is great when you know that each year there is a repeated hiring activity which then stops. They provide flexibility and possess organizational knowledge they carry forward from assignment to assignment. Some may be offered reduced benefits, which are earned based upon how much the employee is needed. They are good candidates for unexpected future FTE growth for the HR department.

- **Part time** – If you have a need for talent but candidates need to work reduced hours for personal reasons, this is a great alternative. Top performers can be put into positions of need tailored to their strengths. Your company gets maximum impact in the time they produce without incurring FTE labor costs. You can also use this in a "try before you buy" scenario. You can hire them before you know you have a need and either convert them to FTE or VSP as future business needs warrant. They may be eligible for reduced benefits based upon hours worked and they would not lose any tenure with your company. This gives you a labor pool to pick from in the future when the candidates' needs change. If there is a downturn in demand, they can be let go or have their hours reduced without any approvals or justification.

- **Recruiting process outsourcing (RPO)** – Some companies try to outsource whole departments or teams, but the companies enjoying the best success are the ones which only outsource high-volume positions. They will outsource high-volume activities such as advertising, data entry, and candidate management. They will then turn over any qualified candidates from this pool who are moving to the interview stage to the full-time recruiters for further facilitation of the recruiting process. RPOs are best used in high-volume, location-specific roles where the outsourcer can benefit from using their scale of operations.

REASONS FOR CONSIDERING RPO SOLUTIONS:

- They possess all the necessary job-board licenses and software, which are expensive to purchase yourself.
- They can be contractually managed to meet certain benchmarks and source data to compare your efforts to other companies.
- Better reporting can be built into their process so you start to learn about which websites are successful without having to go through procurement processes for each individual one.
- They must train and manage resourcing during the project, saving your company from the equipment cost and lost productivity from attrition within your recruiting team.
- Outsourcing is an effective way to move other tasks with little disturbance to the recruiting team. Once an outsourcer knows your company, they can perform a plethora of tasks (such as job fair attendance and training sessions) which are important but time consuming and low in required expertise.
- They provide benchmarks so you can see how you are performing compared to competitors. Some offer specific recruiting/hiring-team training to help you to improve your operational areas and develop best practices from other clients to use for your organization.
- You can "ring fence" the costs of the vendor and assign

> it directly to the project. They provide you with a pre-dictable cost model for budgeting purposes and they will not be distracted by other activities. The resources are only used for the projects they are contracted to perform, so you are getting their focused attention.

The disadvantages of outsourcers are they struggle with "one-off" and specialized positions. Their strength lies in volume hiring. They require an account manager from your team to help them to identify and remove organizational roadblocks and policies.

- **Agency recruiting** – Executive search firms are a great way to fill key, specialized positions. They are able to focus in a way internal recruiters cannot. There are several reasons to consider using them for some your company's key roles:

  o They can conduct confidential searches.
  o They can target people or companies your recruiting teams cannot.
  o Your company can benefit from the market data they can provide on an ongoing basis.
  o They have some connections that can assist in identifying passive candidates.
  o They are a great way to find candidates in very niche markets, allowing your recruiting team to focus on the positions where they can leverage economies of scale.

  The biggest obstacle to using them is the price. They are very expensive and using them for more than a few positions is cost prohibitive.

  These are the most common resources to be used specifically for hiring. The strength of knowing and using all of them in a planful manner is that the recruiting function can become an agile, strategic function instead of just acting as an administrator of a process.

- **Longer-term project resourcing** – There are many government entities, community outreach organizations, and college programs which can be used to resource long-term project design, allowing the recruiting team to focus on meeting today's hiring requirements.

Some of the groups I have had great success with are as follows:

- **Government agencies** – Several agencies are dedicated to improving the employment opportunities of the community and many will partner with you to help them to maintain and improve their offerings. There are a great number of training, transportation, and counseling resources designed to help if you know who to ask.
- **Colleges and universities** – Departments and professors are looking for real business projects to help educate their students on applying the skills they have learned in class. Some will provide grad students to work on some of your team's most pressing recruiting processes.
- **Internal cross-functional project teams** – Take advantage of current talent and employee development opportunities to allow top performers from other functions to work with top performers in recruiting to solve the various business challenges within your recruiting team. There will be limits to their availability and you will need a lead sponsor to ensure the project maintains suitable priority, but this is a great way to share ideas and to gain allies for the hiring processes across the organization.

The advantage of each of these is that you can gain a new perspective about your company and recruiting process. It will come from different backgrounds and points of view which your company can use to improve most of the processes associated with recruiting. They also help to build your company brand and create relationships that can open additional labor pools for your current and future openings.

THINGS TO CONSIDER:

- How flexible is the resourcing model your company uses within talent acquisition?
- Is it a standard design or do you support your recruiting teams by allowing them to utilize flexible resourcing?
- What accountability measures are your leaders using to improve performance and increase positive results?

If you want to discuss this topic or if you need help designing your processes and programs, go to
https://winningthewarfortalent.org.

7

HOW DOES YOUR PROCESS RUN?

A few months ago, I was speaking to a mentee who was a re-cruiting manager at a major company. He had been having trouble with various steps of his interview process. I asked him how things were going.

He replied: "I was speaking to the director of the business I support. I had been sharing concerns that had been raised by candidates for nearly a year. I just could not convince her our process impacted the quality of the candidates and the time it takes to fill a role. We were taking so long to open, interview, and close a position that many of the candidates were going off the market before we could extend the offer. Then when we did finally extend the offer, it was so low our rejection rates were very high. We were impacting our hiring brand and wasting a lot of effort on candidates we wanted to hire but could not get them hired. She just did not believe there were any problems. I just needed better recruiters and more of them."

When I asked how he had addressed it, he answered: "I did two things. First, I dedicated time in one of our weekly 60-minute check-ins specifically to having her sit down and apply for a current job on her team. It was a very important strategic position, and she was frustrated we were not finding good candidates quickly enough."

I asked how it went. "She was appalled at how long it took her to apply. There were so many steps her interview team was adamant about including that the process was very awkward, and it took 45 minutes to complete the preliminary application. I then did a search for a similar job at another company which was our competition for this candidate. It took her five minutes to complete the process. I then asked, 'You are a top performer; if you were looking for another position, which of these would you apply to?' She took a second to answer and replied, 'Theirs.'"

Using Case Studies to Make Recommendations

Curious to see what recommendations they would make, I presented a basic case study to an MBA team from a top university to look at the requisition process. They had access to our records and data to help answer their questions as they completed their evaluations. We were shocked to hear there were 28 contact points from the time someone wanted to open a requisition to the time a candidate walked in the door. There were many departmental approvals and requests that had to be made. Individually, none were overly time consuming, but combined they became a significant hidden cost to the organization. Multiply those times the 15,000 offers we made in a year, and you start to see a process containing substantial organizational costs while adding little value to the process. In a war for talent, those who can reach the best decisions the fastest will usually win.

Using Surveys

Surveys can be a great way to measure the effectiveness of your staffing process or any of its components. The best companies use a customer satisfaction survey that is centrally monitored and facilitated to get measurable feedback from hiring managers and internal and external candidates. This allows their leaders to see overall performance and performance by position, department, and hiring team. It gives the interview team measurable data to show how each population feels about the process. Using surveys as measurement generators is a powerful way to determine what is going well and where improvements can be made.

The best companies also track this feedback to performance scores so their leaders can start to see trends and establish correlations between the interview process and the performance results of those who complete it. For example, tracking employee performance and comparing it to how the employees were initially assessed is a great measure of the interview process.

Do You Have the Right People on the Team?

As you gather data, you will begin to have new insights. Those insights may result in a re-evaluation of the recruiters and interviewers involved. The decision to make personnel changes can be difficult, especially when it impacts long-term employees. Sometimes it is necessary to move those who can no longer perform a job that is being clarified by data, because the data-driven role may not be of interest to them.

Additionally, finding recruiters who have experience designing and operating in a data-driven environment is a good way to infuse new ideas and to introduce new concepts within the team.

> **Sometimes it is necessary to move those who can no longer perform a job that is being clarified by data, because the data-driven role may not be of interest to them.**

Just because a recruiter cannot do the newly defined job, does not mean they must be terminated from the company. They can be considered for other roles aimed at their interests and strengths such as project manager or other human resources positions. I have also seen where teams have used the efficiencies gained to fund additional initiatives such as internal mobility, diversity initiatives, community outreach, or special projects that can more effectively benefit the company.

Similarly, good employees do not necessarily make good interviewers and assessors of talent. Using the data and observations gathered, some interviewers will likely need to be moved into other roles where they can continue their strong contributions.

THINGS TO CONSIDER:

- When was the last time you applied to a key position on your team? How easy is it to find, and how easy is it to apply?
- Have you ever counted the steps involved in opening, interviewing, and hiring a candidate? Are there any duplicate efforts that could be eliminated?
- Does anyone do a periodic process review to see how things are being handled?

If you want to discuss this topic or if you need help designing your processes and programs, go to
https://winningthewarfortalent.org.

I have provided you with several topics for you to consider about your team's operations. My suggestion is to review a few of them to see how your organization is doing and to provide a baseline of current practices and processes so as we now progress into reviewing the recruiting process, there will be a starting point from which you can prioritize your future process design.

With all of this said, how do we begin? I have broken down the interview process into the following process steps and will discuss challenges, opportunities, and solutions for each.

SECTION 2:
PROCESS EXECUTION

The items presented in Section 1 represent some of the business processes within the interview process. Section 2 is going to examine the steps in the interview process and ways to analyze and improve them. In each chapter, we will follow the story of Jim and Jasmin. We will walk through their conversations and discuss best practices, ideas, and issues associated with each. This is where we will revisit the basics discussed in Section 1 and add the steps to operationalize them.

8

REQUISITION PREPARATION

| Requisition Preparation | Go to Market | The Search is On! | Assessing Talent | Choosing the Best Candidates | Launching Their Career With You |

I was attending a divisional leadership meeting with leaders from some of the businesses I supported. Each leader provided an update on budget, goal attainment, office space needs, and hiring status of the projects they were assigned. Jim was one of the leaders in attendance. When it was Jim's turn to report, it was pointed out that he was behind in several categories, including project status and customer ratings. He was obviously upset and stated, "All of my problems can be traced to one thing, recruiting! The recruiters take three to four weeks to open a requisition and then when the candidates apply, none of them match the job. These are positions we have hired in the past so I do not see why the recruiters can't fill the positions. I have been complaining about this for five years. All the recruiters do is answer the advertising responses and those are not the candidates we want. We either leave the position open or hire terrible candidates who leave after six months. We have been asking for more candidates but all they do is blame the process. We MUST do something right away. My neighbor is a recruiter, and she says they could fill our positions in less time than the 90 days it takes us to do it today."

We were about to move on when Jasmin interrupted. Jasmin

had been a peer of Jim's for six months and she hired candidates similar to Jim's. She started by saying, "I had a similar experience with recruiting when I first started. It was so painful I spoke to the recruiting team. We too had three-to-four-week delays in getting positions open, but we found out it was due to the business approval process. In looking at the job descriptions being used, our hiring managers were using out of date descriptions or descriptions that were so vague, the candidate did not know what they were applying to. The interview team felt like we were attracting the wrong candidates and losing the best of those.

"Once we realized this was bigger than any one thing, we convened a team of hiring managers, recruiters, human resource professionals, and finance. We agreed upon a process where the manager would approve title, level, and compensation ranges with finance and human resources up front. Once this was accomplished, the recruiter and manager would hold an intake session to review the description to be used. The recruiter now opens the requisition and begins recruiting on the same day."

Jim replied, "I have doubts the process is the problem. It sounds like you have the better recruiters and I have the low-performing ones."

I then responded, "No, you both use the same team of recruiters." The vice president asked the three of us to continue the discussion privately and report back on our findings.

Hiring people for your company takes time, energy, and resources. Not only are there direct charges that are visible (advertising costs, strategic memberships, marketing materials), but most of the charges also occur in ways not as visible. Scheduling, re-scheduling, screening, and interviewing all add payroll and productivity costs to the process that most companies do not track. Minimizing the "currency" of time reduces costs to the company and frees time for interview team members to perform the primary aspects of their jobs. Overhead also detracts from the time that can be spent creating an excellent candidate experience. Speed, clarity, and coordination of execution are valued by the candidates, so identifying and removing bottlenecks and road-blocks is very important. It has been proven through the collection of survey data that candidates with a poor experience carry the experience over to their thoughts of your company product and the likelihood of recommending your product to others.

Whenever I hear about the length of time a recruiter takes to open a requisition, I look first at the approval process, starting with preparation. I have often found that according to the hiring manager, the requisition should show up immediately. The challenges occur when there is an approval process with five layers. While each layer takes only a day or so to complete, the cumulative time can average 15 business days. During this time, the amount of email traffic and meeting time is significant. Recruiters spend most of their time answering questions about requisition status for the 30 requisitions they have open and less of their time finding and responding to new candidates. The recruiters also end up shifting their time to the high-volume roles to fill as many positions as possible, whereas the more strategic, harder to fill roles get deprioritized because of the amount of overhead present.

One thing to think about when determining an interview loop for candidates is the level of the candidate. For example, incurring the financial and time costs of a CFO's involvement when filling a finance leader role or a role with key strategic importance to the finance team may be required. However, having the CFO interview for junior contributor roles is not only going to increase the cost associated with filling the position but will also slow down the process. The return on investment of the interview loop members should be taken into consideration when forming the loop. The same concept holds true when crafting offers. Giving some decisions and the accountability that comes with explaining their decisions to lower-level leaders gives them more experience in making offer decisions for the future.

Once a hiring need is identified, there is a great rush to get the job posted so the process can begin as quickly as possible. Investing time at the beginning of the engagement will speed the process up if it is prioritized properly. It will also reduce the amount of effort it will take later in the process. Getting the recruiters, the interviewers, and the hiring manager together and establishing agreements around response times, assignment of responsibilities, and operational parameters will help to reduce the overhead of trying to do all of this as challenges occur.

Charting the Process Timeline

One exercise I have found that really assists in a strategic and operational way involves charting and tracking the time spent in all the stages of the hiring process. As the projects proceed, the recruiting team can start to piece together a timeline that can be used to set appropriate expectations for all stakeholders. Charting the time frames allows for changes to be made based upon the needs of the business. Often, the hiring manager receives instruction to fill the position as quickly as possible. Often this is interpreted as being within the next few days. There are a few components highlighted here, although they may be different for different departments or companies. Some are fixed and some are variable, and they combine to track an accurate estimation of the time to fill. Once a baseline is established, the hiring team can begin to determine how to adjust the process to meet the needs for each position. Once the baseline is established, the team can then compare the actuals to the plan to determine

> **One exercise I have found that really assists in a strategic and operational way involves charting and tracking the time spent in all the stages of the hiring process.**

realistic expectations of the time to fill. Here are some samples of common timeline "costs" to be discussed:

- One week to have the intake meeting, coordinate details, and agree upon the job description, the job level, and pay.
- Two weeks to post the position and source candidates.
- Two weeks to schedule finalists with the interview team.
- One week for all interviewers to attend and conduct their interviews and provide feedback.
- Two-or-more-week notice (depending on level, time of year, and timeline of the work the candidate is currently operating under).
- One week for offers to be approved and the offer letter generated.
- One week if there are any negotiations or questions regarding the position and the candidate.
- One week to check references and conduct any background, drug, or credit checks (depending on position).
- Three to five days for the candidate to accept the offer.
- Three-plus days for the background/drug testing results.

In this example, expecting to start a candidate within anything less than a three-week timeline is unreasonable, and this is known when the process starts. According to the estimates, the candidate will be able to start approximately 12 weeks after announcing the job need. With the information above, you can now begin to discuss which parts can be expedited and which are non-negotiable. The interview teams can then assign tasks and expected timelines to get to a point where they can be shown the timeline for filling the requisition. Having the discussion up front can begin the education and partnership discussions important to the success of the efforts.

The variable timeline "costs" can be changed based upon the situation, level of position, and possibly geographic location:

- Availability of the manager to have the intake session.
- Level of specialization of the position will determine the speed in which candidates can be generated.
- Availability of the interviewers for the interview and for the comparison discussion at the end of interviews. Missed interviews or reschedules can impact this.
- Amount of overhead involved in all levels of the communication between the company and the candidate.
- The ability/willingness to pay based on the external labor market vs. internal equity.

By breaking these times out, it allows all stakeholders to know what the expectations are, and it allows for the measurement of success to occur much earlier in the process. If an organization only judges the effectiveness of the process by measuring hires, then it will be difficult to know if your activities and performance are accomplishing the task without having to wait until the requisition is filled. By communicating at each stage of the process, you can begin to predict success much earlier and the team can adjust on an ongoing basis instead of waiting until the position is (or is not) going to be filled within the agreed upon time frame. A form, which has been useful in building partnerships and in streamlining the process based upon the data collected through the automated recruiting reporting, can be found at https://winningthewarfortalent.org.

Make it Systems Based

Data is important, but limit the type and amount of data to what the information systems you use can produce. If you think of a recruiter's time in terms of production capacity, you do not want them spending their time on reporting. Limit the reporting to the information which can be systematically supported and seen by key stakeholders. Every minute a recruiter spends manually creating a report or answering a question takes time away from finding and interviewing candidates. You also want the cumulative data captured for the organization for possible future use. If recruiting assignments change or recruiters leave, your company does not want to lose the data they gathered. The data is created using dashboards or scorecards independently monitored by all involved. Invest in the systems for the automation to make the data gathering quicker, easier, more accessible to key stakeholders, and longer lasting, and you will have much better results.

Skills-Based Job Postings

Job postings are an important part of the hiring process. They are used to serve as a statement of record regarding the role requirements and the explanation of the position. This presents a bit of a challenge in some cases because they are primarily recommended by HR and are designed to comply with labor and employment guidelines.

The challenge is that job postings require an explanation of the qualifications for the role. The tendency has become to quantify items that do not really demonstrate the qualifications necessary to be considered for the role. Unfortunately, this has turned into listing items that make certain assumptions about a person's qualifications but do not really get to the heart of what is needed in the position. It results in a higher number of applicants who may fit the stated criteria but are not good for the role. Reviewing this increased number reduces the time available to locate the candidates who are qualified and uses resources inefficiently without improving the outcome.

The charts below are an example of a job description for a manufacturing company.

SAMPLE POSITION		
SALES REPRESENTATIVE	**SUMMARY OF "EXPERIENCE NEEDED"**	**PROPOSED POSSIBLE QUALIFICATIONS**
KNOWLEDGE, SKILLS & ABILITIES		Bachelor's Degree or Commensurate experience
Required Education:	Bachelor's /Undergraduate Degree preferred	Demonstrated knowledge within the building materials industry
Field of Study Preferred:	Marketing, Engineering, Business	Must have successful sales/business development experience in the commercial building materials sector.
Required Work Experience:	At least 5 years of successful sales and/or business development experience in building materials	Must demonstrate the ability to conduct unsolicited sales calls and be able to demonstrate the ability to communicate up to the Director level in one to one and one to many settings
		Must be able to show a history of collaboration with other departments within the company.
		Must demonstrate customer focused problem-solving skills involving complex scheduling and shipment coordination.

In the first column, it shows the posting as it is listed today. On the right is an example of skills-based descriptions. These contain some of the items describing the qualifications required to perform the role. By identifying the key components of the role, the ability to assess the basic qualifications of the role can be automated. As we have previously discussed, automation allows for all applicants to be considered using the same criteria. Automation is an enabler, and it should be made clear to the applicant that a recruiter is making the decisions regarding next steps and the program is simply gathering the information for comparison by a human in a consistent way.

Having a clear job description accurately outlining the requirements of the position can help to reduce the number of unqualified candidates who apply. As time goes on, if the requirements of the role do not change, the amount of time to complete the requisition preparation stage will decrease.

Interviewer Cost of the Interview Process

So far, the discussion has centered around the pre-hire logistics, the impact it has on hiring, and the impression of your brand from the candidate's perspective. Now let's talk about the interview process itself from a financial and business perspective.

Even with companies who have their own recruiters, a huge amount of the time is spent in getting to the point where a hire can be made. If not monitored, you can easily expend more energy than a position is worth. This costs the company production time for the individual departments, including the recruiters. We will talk about how the volume impacts the quality of the candidate pool in Chapter 9, but here we want to assess the impact that the interview process can have on efficiency and how the planning of it can help to reduce those costs.

Number of Candidates	Number of Candidates
7	4
Hourly Cost Commitment per Interviewer per Candidate	Hourly Cost Commitment per Interviewer per Candidate
$100	$100
Time Commitment per Interviewer per Candidate	Time Commitment per Interviewer per Candidate
2	2
Total Time Cost per Interviewer per Candidate	Total Time Cost per Interviewer per Candidate
$200	$200
Total Interviewer Cost per Candidate	Total Interviewer Cost per Candidate
$1,400	$800

The table on the left illustrates a typical interview schedule. As mentioned previously, for some positions interviewing more candidates is necessary. Senior positions or positions relying heavily on interacting closely with other departments and collaborating with a wide variety of people at various levels within the organization may be worth this type of investment. There are also studies that clearly show the number of interviewers for most positions is not reflected in candidate performance. Scheduling and organizing large interview teams adds to time to fill and additional expenses tied to scheduling and logistics. For candidates from out of town, travel costs and schedule availability will also increase the costs of filling these positions. Again, for low volume, strategic roles, this may very well be the best way to approach the hire. As we will see in the table on the right, the difference between this approach and a more concentrated approach can be significant.

The chart on the right illustrates how the interview process decisions can impact the cost of interviewing significantly. The simple act of reducing the number of interviewed candidates to four from seven can cut the cost of filling the position by over 50%. The smaller number is easier to manage, and the assessments can become much more consistent and of better quality, especially when each interviewer is assigned specific skills to cover.

It is also important to look for scenarios where the company's hiring is going to take place for the lower-revenue-generating positions. Applying this approach to lower-cost, higher-volume roles results in the savings becoming much more significant as the volume increases. Often these are the positions either directly tied to sales or closely relevant to the success of the sales team. Not only does any overhead in the process increase costs in these positions, but their vacancy can negatively impact revenue-generating activities.

Major corporations with successful hiring initiatives are discovering that some of the highest performers were found when the hiring teams successfully switched from pedigree to duty-based job descriptions. Skills-based interviewing is also resulting in much more internal mobility because the skills needed are not unique to one department.

Functional Positions

Some companies require hiring leaders to monitor headcount as a method of cost control. Headcount numbers are important, but if an organization creates functional positions without changing the way the headcount is monitored, it can have unintended negative consequences. Having a lower headcount requires a leader to get more out of each person. That drives costs up because senior team members are more expensive than a person who can perform the lower levels of the tasks needing to get done. Team performance slows down and causes dissatisfaction among senior team members who must spend significant time completing the administrative or lower value activities being assigned to them.

Utilizing functional positions more efficiently is a way I have seen companies solve the situation. Hiring less experienced people to do the lower-level work allows them to concentrate on it and innovate due to their ability being more suited to lower-level work. In some cases, those positions can cost half of what a senior specialist makes, so you can invest in the administrative tasks while also increasing bandwidth for the specialized roles. Moving from headcount-based reporting to payroll-cost reporting allows both groups to benefit. Both are being utilized in ways matching their skills and interest and this allows for the quality of output from all members of the team. The companies moving to this approach are creating a future pipeline for more senior positions as the lower-level employees build their competence.

THINGS TO CONSIDER:

On a scale of one to ten, with ten being the highest score, how would you rate your organization in the following areas:

- The job descriptions accurately reflect the skills required to be considered for the role.
- The interview team's awareness and agreement on what those qualifications are.
- The interview team's ability to consistently recognize candidates who possess those qualifications.
- The correlation of the level of the interview team and the value the position provides.
- In addition, has your company looked at moving from headcount-number reporting to salary-expense reporting?

Go to https://winningthewarfortalent.org for additional information and articles on this topic.

9

GO TO MARKET

Requisition Preparation > Go to Market > The Search is On! > Assessing Talent > Choosing the Best Candidates > Launching Their Career With You

In the first follow-up meeting with Jasmin and Jim from Chapter 8, Jim started with his concerns. "We have to hire 90 people in 100 days and the recruiters will not be able to deliver on the commitment."

I enquired: "OK, we have already discussed the pre-work has to happen. What is the budget for additional resources to make this happen more quickly?"

Jasmin interjected: "We worked with recruiting and finance to estimate the true hiring needs and expected timing of the hiring to determine the resources we needed to meet our goals. We factored in an attrition rate for the next six months and for a 'no-show' rate for the first 30 days. The information allowed us to plan on hiring an accurate number. Then we relied on the recruiting team to execute the plan, report back on a weekly basis, and hold everyone accountable for meeting each of their deliverables. We also used the dashboard function of our applicant tracking system so anyone could see the results of our efforts in real time. There was a need to calculate how many hires we must make to fill those positions. We learned based on past efforts, 30% of those hired leave in the first 30 days of employment. We had to factor these items into our hiring calculations."

I then added, "The planning process we utilized also considered timing and flexibility regarding location."

Jasmin shared: "The thing helping us a great deal was creating the practice of designing processes that could be tracked using data. This allowed us to make changes in our location decisions and helped us to change support levels as necessary. For example, we found that providing administrative support to the hiring efforts allowed our schedule owners to manage the meeting and update logistics so the recruiting team could focus on recruiting and assessing talent.

"Once the organization has had the pre-requisition meeting with the interview team to discuss process, ownership, and logistics, we want to proceed to creating the skills-based job postings which will help us to attract the correct candidates for the position."

> **A common mistake some companies make is that they think of hiring in terms of simple arithmetic. They want to increase the talent to 100 so that number is what they plan to hire.**

Agreeing to How Many Positions Really Need to Be Filled

A common mistake some companies make is that they think of hiring in terms of simple arithmetic. They want to increase the talent to 100 so that number is what they plan to hire. If you look at the chart below you will see an illustration of what I am speaking about.

Beginning HC	100		
Ending HC	200		
		INCREMENTAL HC	100
Historical Attrition	20%		
Historical Churn	20%		
			40
		TOTAL ESTIMATED HIRING NEEDS	140

In the above example, I have kept the math easy so you can see what I am showing here. It can be scaled up or down. If you want to grow your team to accomplish a specific result, you must take into consideration the other pieces of the headcount puzzle. As you can see from the chart, using the sample simple data provided, to grow headcount by 100 people (we call this incremental headcount) you must also take into consideration the historical averages of attrition (people leaving the company) and churn (people leaving this team to go to another team within the company). When this is handled correctly, it can help the company to better plan and resource the recruiting team. If these are sales-generating positions, you will be able to add some of the people today who will be needed to deliver the business results needed tomorrow. This also helps the new hires to grow their current business career while positioning them to grow into bigger positions in the future.

Many leaders I have spoken to initially dismiss this calculation because they argue the scale only works for large companies. This is not true. While large companies can benefit greatly because of the scale of hiring, small companies can benefit too. A single vacancy in a small company may have more of a negative impact on business results because of the relative impact it can have on the company. A larger company can absorb inefficiencies at a higher level, but the negative impact exists at companies of all sizes.

What can happen if you don't plan for churn and attrition? The interviewers and hiring managers start to focus on the incremental headcount growth because filling those positions holds the highest priority. In the process, they let other candidates who could do the job in the future go away without further contact.

There have been numerous examples where we were able to partner well with the interview team and hire all who were qualified. We then trained the pool of candidates and moved them into our performance management systems. The thinking here is, for certain positions in certain locations, there would always be a reasonable headcount need. In those scenarios, it was believed we could train them better than if they went on the market. We could begin to move them into billable positions, generating the revenue needed to cover the small cost of over-hiring in the short term. When we then needed them, they were well trained and ready to fully produce, thus reducing the ramp-up time and maximizing the revenue generation capacity of those who were pre-hired. This also improved the financial performance of the company because talent acquisition was no longer acting as an administrative function. Talent acquisition was becoming a viable business and revenue-generating function.

One of the easiest ways to improve the satisfaction and performance of the entire hiring process is to provide guideline protocols for opening a requisition, determining the offer components, and gaining approval to make the offer at the time of opening the requisition.

Creating Standards with Escalation Protocols

One of the easiest ways to improve the satisfaction and performance of the entire hiring process is to provide guideline protocols for opening a requisition, determining the offer components, and gaining approval to make the offer at the time of opening the requisition. Managing the offer process can be an incredibly complex exercise.

Once a hiring manager approaches the recruiting team to open a requisition, their expectation is that the requisition is then open, and candidates are applying immediately. In some companies, this may be true. In others it is not, and it causes a resource cost that most leaders will never see. In one case, we were constantly fighting because the hiring needs were not being met in a timely manner. Other employees were informing their networks of positions, and everyone was checking in with each other to find out when the roles would be open. The opening of the roles was being held up by layers of administrative approvals for a position that had already been approved. If anything changed with the qualifications of the positions, all the changes would have to be re-submitted for approval. Once we were able to organize the data, we could see that it took approximately three weeks to get a position approved and then another three weeks to get all the approvals to make the offer. Using the data and partnering with various stakeholders involved, we were able to get the number down to one day. If the position fell outside of guidelines, it could take longer, and for some positions it will, but by noticing all the positions were falling into this category, we were able to reduce the time to post and fill and it had a positive impact on positions across the company. We were able to spend the time saved to see where we needed to improve in our attraction investments and in other projects which then resulted in the continuously improving productivity of the group.

Pay and Role Duties

Over the last few years, there has been a movement among various governmental agencies to post the salary range for open positions. There has been pressure to require companies to do the same. Posting the starting salary ranges adds transparency and allows companies to focus on the skills of the candidates. Then, combined with clarity on what you are really looking for in a candidate to be successful, you can begin to minimize the risks of pay inequity which is becoming a hot topic in today's economy. If a person is qualified for the role and is satisfied with the pay range posted, they ought to be considered for the role. Caregivers and older workers often complain they will not even be considered because they are "overqualified" for a position. The definition of career has changed and candidates are more interested in receiving things other than just salary and prestige. When your company accepts the concept that some people want to continue to advance their career but in ways that are less traditional, you will do a better job of providing a beneficial employment environment for higher-skilled workers. You will also benefit by truly maximizing the talent value of your workforce with no additional costs. You will also be able to more accurately forecast the cost of adding labor to support organizational hiring activities. Your organization will be winning the Talent War.

Geographical Location

One of the final things that must be considered is the concept of geographic location. In this section, I will provide a few definitions to be more specific about what we are talking about because each of these has some strengths and weaknesses. It is also important to communicate the serious intentions of the company regarding location preferences. If there are 50 local qualified candidates, is the company really going to hire someone remotely over someone with lower skills who is local? Here are the most common terms I suggest using:

- Work from home
- Remote workers
- Work from a centralized location

Let's look at each of these individually:

o Work from home – Someone who is assigned office space in a central location but has some flexibility to work elsewhere as the schedule and their performance allows is considered to be working from home. This may be used for employees who must work after hours or on weekends due to event schedules and location. IT, telephone, and office support services are made available to them when they are in the office and that is where they would be expected to go to utilize these services.

o Remote workers – An employee who works from outside of the office, usually at home, is considered a remote worker. Since there is no central support available, there should be very clear guidelines about what is provided by the company and what is expected to be provided by the employee. Are there procedures for supporting a remote worker? An excellent example is that some repairs may require access to the network resources and external support vendors may not be allowed to have that access. What is the policy and practice for getting the employee back to being productive while the issue is being addressed?

o Work from a central location – One terrific way to expand opportunities for employees and for attracting a broader audience is to create central locations away from the central office. Not only can it be used to expand the labor pool, but it can be used to create leadership opportunities and cross-group leadership for those locations.

Applying geographic considerations to support business initiatives – In working with a large corporation within the health-care industry, there was a need to create a method to determine the best locations for regional sites. In the past, the company had primarily added office locations based upon acquisition and even personal preferences of senior leaders. It was a popular way to retain talent, but the locations chosen did not broaden the labor pool much. By creating business-based priority scorecards, da-ta-driven recommendations for new locations were possible and could be supported in a logical way. The process resulted in cre-ating a concept that led to interest in regional company campus environments. To begin, we looked at the five talent areas (for us it was IT, customer support, nursing, actuarial, and corporate lead-ership labor pools) that we felt the business would need to grow to meet our growth goals. Once we were able to do this, criteria were used to narrow the choices. We used a combination of labor, vendor, government data estimates, educational institutional es-timates, and real estate information to put together a scorecard. Some of the types of criteria we agreed upon are as follows:

- Proximity to non-stop flights to the corporate office
- Projected influx of future candidates in the profiles we had identified
- Number of college graduates expected to graduate for those skills for the next five years
- Proximity to Historically Black Colleges and Universities and populations of minority students in local universities
- Proximity to military bases
- Real estate availability and the cost per square foot for commercial real estate
- The availability of property to purchase and design

An impact analysis could then be used to estimate the impact the different cities provided in terms of available candidates for our main positions. The estimated available talent pool when increasing geographic reach was six times as many candidates for those positions than our current model provided. Because of these estimates, we were able to create a true plan and provide the business with talent availability estimates clearly showing the approximate impact to the talent pool co-locating would create.

Having a few target markets with targeted priority positions helped the business to have better control of the candidate pool and allowed the company to be more influential in the local talent developmental activities. Geographic expansion also benefited the organization by creating more local business connections. Organizations pursuing this approach can then form strong local partnerships, utilize public resources, partner with local organizations, and create an excitement in the market about a future labor commitment in the community. Those companies are increasing their chances of winning the war for talent by dispersing growth opportunities and that increases the population it can benefit.

Putting geographic location and positional flexibility into action – Companies choosing to broaden employee flexibility and geographic locations to increase the labor pool are going to have to create a compensation approach which adjusts to the cost of living for the area in question. Otherwise, the employees will be incentivised to move to a higher-cost-of-living center, negotiate their wages up to meet the higher cost of living and then move to a lower cost location. As a result, the impacted employees will be artificially inflating the pay for the positions in cheaper locations. When this occurs, operational costs are going to increase and have an overall negative business impact. This contributes to the challenges of pay equity because employees who can move will start to get paid much more than those who cannot.

Posting of the Position

Data is an important part of all business processes and this is equally true when it comes to posting positions, where you are posting, and what the individual sites provide for you. You also want to know the combined impact of all your sources. These can all be different based upon the types of roles you are focusing on, so there needs to be a mechanism in place to report on it through all the phases of the interview process.

To the extent possible, you want to be able to see the data of the candidate pool at each stage of the process. This will help you to know where your strengths and weaknesses are regarding attracting a broad pool of qualified candidates. Also, some positions require direct sourcing, where you post the position but most of the great candidates must be researched and contacted. There is a risk here that your efforts may start to lean toward one population or another. Being able to post and source for those positions covers the possibility that active candidates who are looking to move can find you and candidates not looking to move also have visibility to the types of roles you have open now and in the future.

If your job posting activities begin to show a skew in one direction in terms of types of candidates generated, you can begin to have your recruiting team broaden or focus the posting activities. I have also done this through local partnerships which can provide you with branding opportunities and consultation services that will help you to best meet the employment needs unique to each population. An advantage to having your processes for some of the roles consistent and predictable is that then they can provide a greater amount of traction in those locations for the non-targeted roles as well.

THINGS TO CONSIDER:

- How do you currently account for attrition and the changing need for resourcing? Is your resourcing process flexible enough to handle variations?
- Who is accountable at the organizational level?
- How does your organization currently handle the possibility of expanding the locations of your company?
- Do your hiring teams pay attention to the candidate-flow data to see if there are disparities for certain populations at each step of your process?

Go to https://winningthewarfortalent.org additional information and articles on this topic.

10

THE SEARCH IS ON!

Finding and Identifying the Right Talent

As the meeting with Jasmin and Jim continued, Jasmin shared more of her experience. "Once we figured out the type of person we needed, the process we were going to run, and the assignment of duties, we were ready to begin looking at qualified candidates."

Jim responded, "Which, by this point, you have lost all the candidates and alienated them. No one likes talking to a computer to get a job."

I shared with the team: "That is a good point, Jim. Automation is used more in the beginning of the process to share information about the company and the team. The purpose is to allow the candidates in the early stages of the process to learn about us and to answer simple, but important, questions. Up until this point, we have focused heavily on the steps necessary to process the requisition. Our goal is to get the qualified candidates into the next step of the process as quickly as possible so that we can spend more time building personal relationships with them while still adding value to those who are not the best fit for our current openings."

Jasmin added, "The feedback has been great. Candidates appreciated the flexibility at the beginning of the process and being evaluated fairly. Our hiring teams share that we are getting better candidates because the time investment is short and the experience is positive, regardless of outcome. At first, we saw fewer candidates because we were screening out those who were unqualified quickly. We were then able to effectively expand into other candidate pools that we may not have otherwise looked at."

> **Poorly written job descriptions waste time and resources and increase the chance of hiring someone who does not meet the actual qualifications of the job, which represents a huge legal risk for most companies.**

Poorly written job descriptions waste time and resources and increase the chance of hiring someone who does not meet the actual qualifications of the job, which represents a huge legal risk for most companies. Making the job description accurate helps to reduce legal risk and minimizes wasted costs inaccuracy can cause in the process. For some positions, the posting process is primarily used to fill government hiring requirements. For others, it is an extremely effective way of identifying candidates who are looking for work. When they are looking for work, you want to make it easier for them to apply and be considered so you can spend less time finding them. For other roles, there must be a much more concentrated effort to contact qualified candidates who are not likely to respond to advertising. In those cases, you must identify who they are and route them to the appropriate position, which they may not have been interested in if you had not reached out.

Candidate Relationships in a Tight Labor Market

Once candidates become interested in exploring new opportunities, they will shop around, so process speed is important. Several labor market surveys have estimated the best talent is off the market within ten business days. Internships, externships, and other types of external mentoring can help you to establish the relationship before there is a need and before the candidate is actively looking for work. By including these candidates in periodic meetings, lectures, and company events, you get to assist in the candidate's development and better prepare them for success in your company. I advocate using aspiring managers and top performers as mentors for the external candidates with the highest potential to build interest in your organization. Include this as a delivery task in the aspiring manager's goals. This encourages the mentors to stay connected in a programmatic way which can be monitored and documented in prospective managers' development and performance plans.

The primary categories of different talent to consider developing pools for are as follows:

- Active candidates
- Employee referrals
- Internal mobility
- Alumni networks
- Passive candidate "direct sourcing"
- Nontraditional and targeted sourcing

The best recruiting teams include strategies to prioritize and address candidates in the relevant categories to increase the candidate pool. The purpose is to create additional pipelines of target talent which will reduce time to fill and appeal to populations other companies may not be targeting.

Let us cover each category in more detail below.

Active Candidates

Active candidates are important because they are the people who saw your ad, know enough about your company to apply for a position, and are interested in being considered for one. They are on the market and are looking at your and your competitors' ads. Mass marketing and targeted marketing efforts are mostly focussed on generating active candidates. Processing the most qualified of these applicants can help to reduce overall time to fill. It allows more of the recruiters' time to be spent also looking at other ways to attract candidates.

Employee Referrals as a Source of Hires

Conventional wisdom within the industry indicates that employee referrals make the best hires within all positions, and many organizations are proud of supporting the concept for good reason. There is little validated performance data showing they are better candidates, but they can certainly shorten the time to interview and there is a great benefit there. The danger here is that interviewers may develop the tendency to overvalue the candidates who are referred and who are like them. The best companies are those continuously using the data gathered throughout the interview process to monitor whether there really is a performance benefit or whether it is more like the "halo effect". The halo effect takes place when people use bias to view performance in a favorable light. The performance may or may not be better, but it is perceived to be more favorable because they are recommended by someone who is successful.

Employee referrals are an important source of hires and top companies want to encourage the organization members to refer those they know, but just assuming that a referral is a better candidate can have a more negative impact than anticipated.

To Pay or Not to Pay for Employee Referrals

There are many ways to reward people for referring candidates who get hired. Some companies reward the efforts by the employees publicly through some recognition by senior leadership. If done consistently and done correctly, this can be very effective. The concept of having employees identify key talent can be considered an important role of all employees and the culture can reflect it. In those cases, the role of every employee is to help make the company a better place to work. This would mean that you would not provide a monetary incentive for having employees complete a task that is required of them. Successful completion of referrals would be reflected in the performance and bonus programs within the company. Non-monetary recognition from key leaders and stakeholders are a great way to reward these efforts.

Some companies have effectively driven referral programs at the enterprise level and paid for every referral meeting certain criteria of identification, longevity, and performance.

In either approach, the desired outcome should be clear, consistent, and emphasized uniformly across the company. The administration of the referral program should be automated to improve accuracy and consistency.

Employee campaigns to help with this can be effective but there are some components that need to be communicated in writing:

- What exactly is the reward and how do you earn it?
- Set a timeframe and title/location limits—be clear about when the program begins and ends, and which locations or job families are eligible.
- What is the necessary process to follow to be considered eligible?
- Make it a marketing piece instead of just an email. It stands out more and adds a different feel to the communication

than just a plain email. It can also be used like any marketing campaign to target specific audiences where it makes sense to do so.

Documentation and Reporting

The documentation processes for any of the employee referral campaigns must be systematic and easy to implement. Manual, spreadsheet-driven documentation can be so tedious it requires a person or group to administer it. A better approach is to have the applicant tracking system do this automatically and just have someone run the program and monitor the reports. Especially when the referral program is tied to a monetary reward, any situation that does not run smoothly causes distrust and negative feelings within the employee community.

Internal Mobility

Internal mobility consists of the training of employees and helping them to grow their career in ways they are interested in and qualified for. Internal mobility should also align to the growth needs of the business.

There are many ways to define internal mobility but here are the main ones:

- **Promotions –** Promotions occur when an organization has trained a high-performing employee to fill a specific position or type of position. For example, companies will create succession plans to ensure they have the talent they need to fill key positions before vacancies occur.
- **Lateral moves –** Lateral moves are a good way to help growing organizations to accelerate their growth. Using top performers from various teams can help to create the

processes, procedures, and practices more quickly than external candidates. A lateral move is one resulting in the employee being moved into roles that are the same level as their current position.

- **Movement to new functions** – When there are top candidates who know specific parts of the business, it is useful to move them into other departments, regardless of level. For example, an HR Generalist may move into a project manager role for one of the teams they support as a generalist. The benefit is that now there is cross-departmental knowledge which can be applied in new ways. This type of movement does not necessarily include lateral moves or promotions.

- **Addressing reductions in force** – When it is necessary for a company to reduce its investment in some parts of a company, the company will usually eliminate positions. It is not unusual to offer external placement services to those impacted. Several companies have designed ways to use this activity to win the talent war by facilitating a move by top performers to other parts of the company. Others take an additional approach of helping still other impacted employees to find positions elsewhere within the companies well. Not only does it help the employees with continuity of benefits, but it can also save the company on the separation costs incurred when employees are separated from the company.

Several of the organizations I have worked with have improved internal mobility. They had found that the hiring managers and candidates felt like the internal candidate application process was too complicated. The best companies utilize performance records, development plans, and areas of specialty to expedite the application process for their own talent. Those criteria are seen as being good predictors of success and using them can shorten the time it takes to identify candidates and interview them to fill the currently open roles. Internal candidates have numerous internal data points to indicate their value to the company and their performance in their current position. Some of the best organizations have recognized this process as a challenge, and so have formed internal recruiting teams. Those recruiting teams can isolate the challenges unique to the internal process and create a quicker, more agile interview experience. This then creates more time for the rest of the recruiting team to focus their efforts on external candidates. As a result, the candidate experience for both internal and external candidates improves. It has worked so well that a Fortune 50 insurance company was able to drive the average days to start from 60 to 30 days, with internals moving much faster, allowing the external candidate process to move faster as well.

The organizations adopting this have learned they can plan to develop and move the best performing internal candidates into their next role, controlling the time to fill by pre-training them for the next available positions. They then focused on replacing only the entry-level candidates, who are cheaper and easier to find, thus further reducing overall costs to the company while also providing trained, successful internal applicants to different parts of the organization.

> If an employee finds it easier to find, apply for, and interview for jobs at other companies than it is for them to find internal opportunities they are qualified for, they will leave. Since replacement hiring can be as high as 60% in some organizations, the opportunity to cut costs and improve morale is significant.

Alumni Networks and Boomerang Websites

One thing beginning to be seen within successful, large corporations is the creation and activation of alumni networks and boomerang websites. Alumni are former employees who have chosen to continue their careers elsewhere. Boomerang employees are Alumni who would consider returning. These companies continue to leverage the mutual benefits that the company and employees have enjoyed, and want to maintain some of the value to the benefit of all parties. Staying connected to people who may consider working with you again or who would refer others to experience the positive environment you have created is very helpful. Not all the candidates will be interested in the same role they held before, and some of these candidates will have gone somewhere else and gained additional skills you will want to capitalize on. If your current candidate experience is positive, even a negative outcome for a returning applicant can help to nurture candidate advocates in the market. Companies have begun to realize that to win the talent war, they must appeal to former employees and their referrals. When potential candidates are doing research, they will find these networks to be positive indicators about working at your company.

An advantage of having alumni networks is that they are extremely flexible. You may create approaches and content to attract all former employees, but you may also only want to focus on certain specialties in short demand. You can be more specific in your messaging and more flexible regarding where you establish these networks and who you include in them. The type of audience may also dictate how you market and curate the content.

Passive Candidates – "Direct Sourcing"

There is a common belief that passive candidates make better candidates than active candidates do. To an extent it may be true. Passive candidate generation is much more attractive because you can contact someone who has not considered your company for employment and by the end of the discussion has changed their mind. It also allows recruiters to become extremely specific about who is being highlighted as a possible applicant for the role. If all you do is expose them to the same process as active candidates, you are wasting time, much of it theirs. On average, once a passive candidate becomes active (they will speak to you about career opportunities), they are highly likely to also check the market to educate themselves on current salaries, and other potential openings. If you just run them through a normal process, you will have lost the advantage you had gained when you originally contacted them. At this point, the organization acting fastest can win if they are willing to pay market prices for the talent now on the market because of the company's efforts.

Since sourcing is a time-consuming process, it is important to be willing to pay market value. It is important to recognize the situation around a passively sourced candidate. The team loves the candidate, agrees they are the type of talent they want to add to the company, and then comes the offer. If the offer is based upon internal equity instead of market value, the candidate may be discouraged. The challenge is that the current team members have not entered the market and so are naturally not going to carry the same premium as someone who has. From the directly sourced candidate's perspective, you called them with an unsolicited call. Current team members will also have other compensation components (benefits, bonuses, equity, accrued vacation) that the new employee will not possess at the beginning of their career with you. You asked them to give up personal or work time to find out more about the role and then when it came time to offer, you offered less than they had requested due to internal equity. This can have a worse impact than not contacting the candidate to begin with.

Offer-accept expectations – The theoretical expectation of the organization is a 100% acceptance rate. If all the proper steps have been followed, there will be very few offer rejections. Periodically checking the organization's offer acceptance ratio will highlight if there is an issue to investigate.

Passive sourcing and more accurate job descriptions may result in fewer candidates going to the screen stage. When your messaging is consistent and clear, more candidates will decide to withdraw from consideration due to lack of interest. Losing an unqualified applicant earlier in the process allows you to amend your approach so you can adjust process, pay, advertising, and budgeting to align them to the proper audience more cohesively. Success is not just measured in how many apply, but how many are qualified as a percentage of the number of people who were called and convinced to apply. This means your team may see fewer candidates for their roles, but having systemic reporting representing this in real time allows your teams to have a better view of what to expect and what needs improvements. It also allows your organization to change the marketing strategy for the groups presented below.

Using Organizational Partnerships and Recognition

One way many companies work toward winning the talent war is to leverage the influence of partner organizations. Such partnerships can be used to strengthen the hiring brand and the product brand within the target audiences. An example would be the use of organization badges. Awards and recognition earned through hiring efforts also strengthen a corporate brand. They support your business goals, so they include any partnership badges, awards details, or testimonials that have been earned, especially those provided by outside affiliation groups. This effort can co-exist with the efforts of your organization's corporate social responsibility efforts. Many of these outreach organizations recognize the large efforts of large companies, but there are plenty of organizations who focus on recognizing small and local efforts as well.

Surveys show that candidates value seeing the company

engage in community initiatives, even if the initiatives do not include them. They like to see what you are doing, and your employees will take great pride in presenting your story throughout the interview process. It can become very uniting and motivating to all involved in the process and for those who are interested in hearing about it.

Once the processes are in place, it is easy to direct them to target under-represented populations. Examples are:

- Veterans and military spouse hiring
- Retiree hiring
- Internships
- Disability hiring
- Partnerships with minority professional organizations
- Partnerships with historically minority-serving universities

These populations often face significant challenges in being suitably employed and so they represent an opportunity for organizations to increase their talent pool in a way their competition may not. All these groups have associations and organizations designed to help employers to leverage these populations most effectively. They will also provide guidance to create and maintain programs to help manage and attract members of these communities and will allow the partnerships to be advertised on corporate career pages.

These are some of the most pressing items to think about as your teams begin their search.

Candidates Research Jobs

With the accessibility of information about your company at an all-time high, it is important to create practices to provide those who are researching you with the most favorable results possible.

Ensuring your careers are clearly listed on your company

website and are easy to find using search engines is important. This is where candidates will go to see minority representation of your leadership teams, product information, the social engagement efforts of the company, and the careers message of the company. As a result, they need to be able to find all of this information quickly and easily.

THINGS TO CONSIDER:

- Does your organization have a process to assess the effectiveness of hiring within the target populations listed here?
- What have you found?
- Do your leaders know what their offer acceptance rate is for their team and are they held accountable for it?
- Is your organization's web presence candidate focused, or is it strictly product focused?

Go to https://winningthewarfortalent.org for additional information, articles, and discussions on this topic.

11

ASSESSING TALENT

Requisition Preparation 〉 Go to Market 〉 The Search is On! 〉 Assessing Talent 〉 Choosing the Best Candidates 〉 Launching Their Career With You

In a follow up meeting with Jasmin and Jim, Jim started to become more curious than combative. He said, "Ok, it sounds like getting more rigorous in our planning and preparation may be able to help us to save money in identifying candidates, but after finding out about our pay, they ghost us. What can be done to improve those outcomes?"

I answered, "Some positions are very pay sensitive. Candidates can be compelled to accept other offers over as little as 25 cents per hour. However, if you spend some time getting to know their motivation for changing positions, your interview teams can focus on the programs, benefits, and opportunities that are much more valuable and important to the candidate.

Jasmin then added, "Yes, by changing our interview techniques and showing the other benefits that also contain a monetary value, the team learned to present the other components of our compensation package. We also started to get a deeper understanding of all the great benefits the company spends money on to compensate all of us."

Closing the Candidates – Understanding Their Motivations

Candidates have many reasons for looking for a new position. In the absence of preliminary closing conversations, many companies focus on using salary expectations as the primary qualifier for discussing a position with a candidate. This approach is understandable, but it ignores the other benefits being provided by your company. It serves to over emphasize salary as the primary reason for joining your organization. Flexible benefits, tuition reimbursement, 401k programs, employee stock purchase plans, health insurance, and mental health benefits are all examples of benefits that may be more important to your candidate than just salary. Leading companies have begun to add personal leave, increased personal holidays, pet insurance, and subsidized programs at preferred vendors. Having all members of the interview team equally emphasize these components is an important step in communicating that joining your organization is valuable in several ways. Many leading companies are beginning to add no-cost or low-cost insurance plans with high deductibles so candidates can better choose the coverage packages which best work for them. Those companies often offer worksheets to candidates so they can more accurately understand the financial rewards available in addition to the salary.

I spoke to a colleague who had recently interviewed with an institution of higher education. She was a great candidate for the adjunct position she applied to, and the interview process was going very well. When it came time to discuss compensation, they let her know they were not paying anywhere near what she was making in the commercial sector. They spent so much time speaking about the lower salary she lost interest and moved on to roles in other companies.

She later found out the job included free tuition to the University for any programs she and her family wanted to pursue. She shared with me, "I am a mother of three children who still need to attend college. Plus my partner and I would like to earn some specific certifications that would further our education and careers. This represented a huge benefit to us, but because the conversation only included monetary components, I was not able to make a fair comparison between this role and others. I felt compelled to take another offer. Although my new role is a great one, I wish I had information regarding the entire package. If so, I may have made a different decision."

Some companies offer subsidized services on dry cleaning, mobile phones and service, gym membership, and childcare. I have seen companies offer free weight-loss program memberships and free air travel and lodging for qualifying employees. If these are presented as part of the compensation package, the company will be able to more frequently attract those who value monetary compensation, but also those who may value other components as well.

Especially in today's hiring environment, physical, financial, and mental health have become important for candidates and their families, but there is often little to no emphasis on the items that are covered and who they are covered for until the offer is made. Getting to know a little about a candidate goes a long way toward being able to focus on those items most important to them. Questions which help to see what is important to the candidate can be used to identify the best matches but also allows the interview team to highlight those areas, providing more value to the candidate regardless of the current interview outcome.

There is also a recognition that the definition of a successful career has changed for many people. It once was measured only in terms of scale, scope of influence, and size of the organization you play a key role in. There are times in a person's career lifecycle where other priorities come into play. Family business priorities, elder or special needs care, and other situations tend to impact what a career means to a person. Overall, if your company is not designing the hiring process to be able to identify those issues, you are not only attracting only candidates who are motivated by money, you also miss the candidates who value other programs that you offer but that you do not spend time discussing in much detail.

The Candidate-Value Proposition

Previously we discussed using automation early in the application process to create a data-driven scenario where people who take the trouble to apply for a job are being asked to apply to others they may be interested in. Using automation at this stage to query candidates about compensation can also be greatly beneficial. Instead of asking for their salary requirements, ask them to rank the importance of the various components of compensation. This would require you to share with them the details of the available benefits for them and would allow them to choose their own priorities. It is also a more positive exercise than just asking what salary they would need to change jobs. Also consider that this is still a high-volume portion of the process. Scale and volume of candidate flow is where you can lose the most money, and it is also where you can save the most. The idea is to create an exercise that finds the best talent for the company and to provide the greatest amount of value to those who choose to pursue careers with your organization.

Getting Started with Interviewing

While the identification of candidates is still going on, the interviews can begin. Those teams that can move quickly can have a huge advantage over those who cannot. If you want to have

access to the best candidates, try some of the following processes to help you:

Set interview days – Set interview days are a great way to
minimize back and forth discussions between manager, recruiter, and candidate, and work well in high-volume roles with little
differentiation between candidates. When the recruiter finds a
candidate who meets the criteria, they schedule the candidate
and start the interview attendance communications with the candidate. Many teams struggle because they spend so much time
speaking to candidates who they will not pursue, but if the automation recommendations are followed, there will be much more
time to invest in the ones they are interested in.

Set service level agreements (SLAs) – When the candidate
pool is small or when the volume of positions is low, having set
days does not help much. It will slow the process down, and, as
we discussed previously, then the candidates will begin to go off
the market. In those cases, your interview team will want to interview as quickly as possible and decide as quickly as possible.
SLAs can be designed for the open positions and will allow your
team to schedule interviews as you find the candidates, and there
are standard windows and response times to keep the process going quickly. The importance of having clear requirements is that
it makes it possible to hire the first person who fits the requirements. This is not always feasible or in the best interest of all, but
if you do this with the lower priority positions, then the recruiting
team has the bandwidth to communicate clearly what next steps
are and update the candidate as necessary.

Set interview teams – I have seen great successes using dedicated interviewer teams which include interviewers from related
functions where possible. I have had the hiring managers and recruiter partner pick three to five core areas to cover with specific
questions to be covered. In this way, someone is available to cover
each area at any time. Over time, you may use your more senior
interviewers to participate in broader interview activities as their
skills improve.

From a candidate perspective, these processes show that your team was prepared, and the candidate is not wasting their time answering the same questions for every conversation. It also provides the candidate the chance to ask the questions they need to ask in order to come to a decision about working for you.

> Many recruiting teams want to wait until they get three to five qualified candidates to speak to. It is a great way to ensure accurate comparisons, but in this war for talent the average candidate can be off the market in less than five days. You may have your teams rethink the timeline. For senior positions and positions relying heavily on collaboration, this may not be able to be addressed, but for other positions in the organization, the timing and practices are often influenced by habit. Expecting great candidates to wait for five to six weeks for others to have time to go through the process is going to present ongoing challenges. Look for ways to reduce this to beat your competition and win the war for talent.

When hiring for positions within my own recruiting team, at the end of the interviews I like to meet with the candidates briefly to close them and encourage them to consider positions available now and in the future. I met with a candidate recently who was much more reserved at the end of the process than at the beginning of the process. The change was dramatic, so during this last conversation, I asked her why. After a few minutes of hesitation, she finally shared that she was not sure she was a great fit for the position. When I asked her why, she explained that every interviewer had asked her in-depth questions about dealing with hostile leaders in an aggressive environment.

The group she would support was a great partner, and the assignment was a great match. It was also a growing team and was a high-priority group in a fast-paced environment and this was why she was being asked about her experience with conflict resolution. Since everyone asked the same questions, it seemed to indicate a great deal of conflict in the role. She also felt little time was allowed for other conversations. She felt like the team was unprepared. They did not allow her to present all her experiences and she did not have the chance to get a great feel for the environment other than that it was clearly filled with conflict. She was a great candidate with all the experience and personality that fit the profile, but because everyone asked the same questions about a specific topic, she decided to pursue something more consistent with what she wanted to do. She pulled herself out of the process and was not interested in speaking to us again.

Structured Interviewing

Assigned competencies and consistent questions help the organization to minimize the risk by reducing bias in the process. The organizations with the best results assign topics and consistently cover them for every candidate. It does not have to be a complete script, but there are some basic questions that should be consistent for each competency. You will want to be able to truthfully tell the candidate and stakeholders that they were consistently and fairly assessed, and you want to follow federal hiring guidelines by being able to show the criteria being used to make this determination.

There is also a business value to this part of the process. Having all the interviewers conduct interviews accurately and consistently is key to growing the business. Poor execution of this part of the process can hurt your hiring brand in the market and within your team and can inhibit your ability to grow like you need to. Here are some items to consider to improve your results and help you win the war for talent.

Candidate feedback – If companies get candidate feedback, it is usually in the form of anonymous surveys after the interviews and in some cases, these occur several weeks after the interview.

This gives a good macro-picture of satisfaction, but the interview team loses the power of real-time feedback which could be used to improve the interview process in the moment and across time. Your competition who is doing this well is beginning to find ways to gather this feedback in real time. Those organizations are using it to monitor how the candidate feels about the process during the interview. There are several survey applications which can communicate simple and quick feedback immediately after the interview. It can be as simple as a smiley face system with a text box, or a quick numeric rating system. It allows for an intervention or modification of the interview in process based upon the candidate's input. The hiring leader could either switch interviewers or change some of the focus of the next interview based upon this feedback. Over time, the leader would begin to be able determine who are the best and worst interviewers on the team.

Top professionals who interview have the technical skills to perform their job. Unless they are hired specifically to interview people though, it may not be one of their strengths. Since all interviewers' performances are key to the company's hiring successes, any improvement in the experience of the candidate is important. Feedback being delivered quickly and briefly can go a long way to improving the overall impact to the candidate and the interview process.

Process audits – An approach that can also be used effectively by top interviewing teams is the use of an "audit" person. If anyone sees something in the process they question, they can notify the auditor of the process who can then intervene. Auditors can help to resolve process or assessment issues and can make suggestions if the situation warrants it. Keeping the auditing process simple and agile allows for flexibility to quickly address a wide variety of issues as they occur. The simplicity and flexibility make it effective for organizations of all sizes.

Costs of the process – The costs of the process have been discussed throughout the book thus far but we are going to spend a little time talking about them in a more programmatic way. Most of the reporting we mention is backward looking and this is no exception. The difference here is you can look at this with more frequency and it is a good initial indicator of how a function is doing on an ongoing basis. It can also be used to forecast future costs for the business.

Cost of hire – There are several ways to calculate this number and a lot depends on what you are trying to accomplish:

- If you are looking at the bigger picture, you may include recruiter salaries, all of the licenses and marketing costs, and all other costs of candidate travel and expense reimbursement for all recruiting activities. This is a good measure of the macro costs associated with the process. It is generally used for high-level reporting since it really does not provide enough detail for the items that will allow you to manage the process in ways we will discuss in the next paragraph. It is good for big-picture budget creation and for reporting to senior leaders regarding the costs of recruiting. You can use the prior year's costs as a base and then compare more recent monthly details to see a comparison. It is not great for changing future costs and while it can be an initial indicator of information that you can then dive deeper into, it is general in nature.

- A process that you may find more useful from a team management perspective is to consider the recruiting salaries, licenses, and subscriptions at a fixed cost that become sunk costs if hiring volume goes down. This is a "pay to play" model. There are some things that you must do just to be able to enter the talent market, regardless of hiring volume. Social media is a great example. You need a career presence on the various sites and that cost will need to be available on an ongoing basis. Some licenses, partnership affiliations, and the system maintenance of an applicant tracking system (ATS) are also examples of this. The variable costs that are driven by activity such as advertising purchased in advance, candidate travel costs, recruiter salaries, and any other incidental expenses would be included here as well. The best way to manage this for most companies is to use total costs per year, quarter, and month and then divide it by the number of hires that started that month. The downside of this approach is that it omits some costs that are incurred now that will not be recognized until the candidates are hired. It also includes candidates hired that incurred the costs above in a previous month.

Candidate "Pull-Through" Reporting

One challenge that presents itself is in determining the metrics to see how hiring initiatives are doing and using that to predict patterns and adjust based upon those predictions. Historical reporting is good and can be useful, but when you can combine that with some forward-looking reporting, the information becomes much more powerful. Using technology to create the funnel information that we discussed in Chapter 2, companies can track the percentage of candidates that pass through each of the major stages of the process (application, screen, interview, offer, accept).

The best recruiting organizations focus on the "pull-through" reporting to assess the effectiveness and efficiency of their hiring process. They monitor each step and set goals at each so that they can identify issues as they occur. As the activity gets closer to offer, the cost to get candidates to the next step cumulatively increases. As a result, the pull-through metrics become more heavily prioritized as the process continues. As a shortcut, top organizations give priority to the pull-through metric of the ratio of offers/accepts. The best organizations target an offer acceptance rate of 93% and above. They feel that this ratio represents a good alignment and a process that is highly effective. It captures the standard offers while also showing that some people will change their mind due to counter offers, geographic location, or other components that they learned about during the offer process.

The organizations that struggle the most often have it show up in the offer/accept ratio. The lowest ratio that I have seen is one where 45% of all offers are accepted. Financially, it means that they will be spending more money and time than their competition for the talent that they are hiring. Seeing this as a metric allows them to start looking at each stage to see where problems may be occurring.

On several occasions, I've been faced with high hiring needs and a limited amount of time. The anxiety among the stakeholders was high and a great deal of valuable recruiting time was spent discussing progress or lack thereof. For most companies, the average time to fill a high-volume position is approximately 60–90 days. We did not have that long, so I created a dashboard with the applicant tracking system that we were using. It showed me the historical information regarding the percentage of candidates of each stage that advanced to the next stage. We also tracked the historical amount of time a candidate was in each stage of the interview process. We were able to create agreements that in the future we would reduce the amount of time at each stage and determine an approximate yield of all the current activities. In this way, we were tracking metrics within the first week and adjusting our approach as we progressed so that we were able to meet the targets. It required a good understanding of the expected yield at each step of the process and contributed to a closer partnership between the hiring manager and recruiters. This resulted in the business having more confidence in their ability to handle the volume, and removed resource and process roadblocks that would otherwise slow down hiring activities and keep us from meeting the business goal.

The benefit to this approach was that it was flexible and could be produced by any of the key stakeholders in an automated way. We were all looking at the same data in the same format without manual manipulation, which takes so much time and risks incorrect or incomplete data.

THINGS TO CONSIDER:

- Has anyone in your organization checked on the interviewing processes being used? Have they identified and prioritized the activities that would lower the cost of the process while improving the outcomes?
- Is your organization using service level agreements and projected timelines to plan for hiring?
- Are you using the data captured by the applicant tracking system to see how the team is performing and making decisions to improve outcomes?
- Are you ensuring that your interviewers are using structured interviews?

Go to https://winningthewarfortalent.org for more information on this topic.

12

CHOOSING THE BEST CANDIDATE AND CLOSING THEM

Requisition Preparation > Go to Market > The Search is On! > Assessing Talent > Choosing the Best Candidates > Launching Their Career With You

When we met again, Jim was beginning to understand what Jasmin and I had been sharing with him. He started the conversation with, "I have given a lot of thought to what you have been saying. I have come to realize that we had created parts of the interview process at different points in time. Over time, they had become less efficient than I had realized. When we started having conversations with all involved and compared it to the process components that Jasmin has used with her team, we realized that we should look at things differently. When the leaders started to see the collective waste of time that had been generated across the organization, they became curious. When they saw the data that had been captured, they were alarmed. Just think of what we could be doing if we were hiring a higher percentage of the candidates that we interviewed. We would be interviewing fewer people in person and hiring more of them while also giving them a better experience."

Jasmin added, "Yes, and in an environment where anyone was disgruntled with any part of the process, they can rate you low on public review boards. Cutting down on that may mean hiring less with a higher percentage of those interviewed being hired and retaining them more successfully."

That is a key point to make because it applies to every company, regardless of industry, size, or business cycle. You can determine if that is consistent with your company's performance by looking at the data. Since we have shown so far that waste and therefore costs are tied to volume, if you improve the efficiency of hiring, you can reduce the processing costs and either reduce the number of recruiting resources needed, or invest in the programs that can be used to create further savings and better developmental programming for your employees.

Once a company can get comfortable with the concepts of targeted advanced hiring, the same can be applied to growth areas within the company. I am often surprised when I hear about a team that is proud of their hiring efforts because four great candidates who can do the job well were identified. They are planning to make one offer for the position that they have open. When I ask about hiring more, their response is that they do not have an open requisition. The reaction is understandable since the manager has a strict limit to headcount. Basically, they are going to make three candidates unhappy with the process. Especially for revenue-generating positions, the cost of a few months of salary will be positively offset by the increased sales revenue. At some point, going up the organizational structure, I will find the senior leader and mention it to them, and rarely have they rejected the opportunity to get ahead of hiring. They are also likely to have many positions open which are not likely to be filled in the short term. Early hiring, whether with internal or external candidates, can have a dramatically positive business impact on the organization, but some front-line managers do not understand it. Most executive leaders will, so building the rapport with the executives was a key for me to be able to influence this decision at their level.

Here are some of the things we took into consideration when crafting offers:

- Qualifications of the candidate. Why did you call them at the beginning of the process?
- What do they bring to the table? Do not be afraid to show appreciation for it.
- What are their priorities and how does your role meet them?
- Don't assume they know why you want to offer them the position. Share anything that stands out to you or anything special you have planned for them to contribute to. Also include a realistic timeframe of when developmental activity may begin.
- Give them examples of how you have delivered proven benefits to other people in their roles, where you have advanced their careers, and how.
- Verify the general priorities which will be undertaken with them in the long and the short term. Let them know you have a plan, even if you do not have all the details of it. Help them to start to visualize what working with you will be like and how it will benefit them.
- Utilize the compensation guidelines agreed upon to reduce the time it takes to create the offer details.
- Communicate to the candidate how the entire package meets all the needs the candidate indicated at the beginning of the process. Make it bigger than just the money.
- Maintain a candidate focus. When the phone rings and a candidate has a question, ensure that your teams are moving past the tendency to say, "That is not my department," or, "That is not my job," and into the practice of saying, "Let me help you to get the information you need."

Recruiter and Manager Roles

Recruiters and managers both have critical roles in the offer process. It is important that they understand what those roles are so they are presenting a unified front to the candidate. I have found it best when there is a script the recruiter uses when presenting the offer and then a more fluid conversation regarding other components. By having the person who is recruiting and the manager oversee different portions of the activity, you are allowing for some degree of negotiation and offer-review which are consistent and quick. This also helps to avoid situations where the candidate feels like they received different information during the offer stage than what they experience once they start.

Tip

Especially in cases of specialized or highly skilled workers, it is important to be able to show what was discussed if questioned about it later. For these candidates, it is safe to assume they are receiving a great deal of information from various companies and conversations. It is easy for them to misremember the details. Our practice was to have the recruiter use the offer letter as the script. The entire letter does not have to be read, but the specifics relevant to the position are outlined and specifically presented. Then the manager can follow up with a call to answer additional questions. If a negotiation is requested, the manager could ask to consult with the recruiter and their leaders, especially if the details requested are outside the parameters agreed to ahead of time.

As we have previously discussed, most of the high-volume positions can be efficiently managed using pre-approved offer details. At all levels, these should be handled consistently. Examples are listed below:

- Compensation range
- Modifiers for certifications, shifts, or language skills
- Standard vacation and benefits
- Signing bonus requests
- Performance-based bonus structure
- Equity awards

- Other benefits such as extra time off
- Timeline commitment requests, such as upcoming trips or personal commitments

The role that internal equity plays in hiring cannot be overstated.

Some of these will be non-negotiable, regardless of the position. Base levels of benefits and annual bonus may be examples of this. It is important to note, even in cases where there are agreements in place, that it is not to be seen as being policy. There are practices, which are flexible, and policies, which are not. Guidelines are in place which recognize that while most candidates are going to receive the approved standard offer, extraordinary candidates will likely require extraordinary concessions. These guidelines allow flexibility for hiring managers to request those exceptions with justification. It is the role of the recruiter to see that the appropriate guidance is being given and the appropriate conversations are occurring within the business. The recruiter will facilitate and support the decision, but the decision and details are to be handled by the hiring manager and their leadership teams to ensure an appropriate and consistent process is being followed. The partnership between all stakeholders is very important for all involved because all will pay the consequences of a misstep. Being able to solve the challenges in a unified way will impact the performance of the interview team in the future.

Internal Equity

The role that internal equity plays in hiring cannot be overstated. Consider the following common occurrence as an illustration of what I mean. A business requests that their recruiting team find passive candidates who are not yet on the market and who are excelling in their current positions. The expectation is that the recruiter finds candidates who represent an upgrade or add experiences not reflected in the current talent of the team. The recruiter contacts them and gets them interested in the position, but now the candidate becomes active. They are shopping around to see what else is out there. They have been moved from premier talent (that demands top dollar) to a candidate on the open market (which also demands top dollar due to low supply). The company invests in all of the costs and processes described here and are excited to offer the candidate. The interview and stakeholder teams agree that this is a great potential hire. Often, instead of offering what the candidate has clearly demanded, the hiring manager wants to offer less because their current team makes less than what the candidate is asking. There are three things that come to my mind when I see this happening:

- We have found exceptional talent; we need the talent, and we now know the market value of the talent. If we need the talent enough to start the search, we need to be prepared to pay a premium for the candidate.
- The management team needs to be united in explaining why, in case it is questioned by other team members.
- There should be a plan to create parity with the current high performers or else they will leave to receive market value for their skills.

Offers and Cutoff Dates

One thing to remember is most companies will have a cut-off date for new hires to be considered for the next performance assessment. Anyone who starts after the cut-off date will not be eligible for salary, bonus, or equity considerations until the following year. Even if there is no cutoff, the expectation is that proven performance components of new hires are going to be less than those who have been there the whole year. Even if the new hire will eventually perform at a higher level, which may take some time and will not be fully realized in the first performance cycle. In this case, you are basically considering that the new hire will be compensated for this gap in increases up front since they will not be in full participation in the compensation plan for an extended period. Also, any effect tenure has on benefits or particularly equity must be remembered when comparing the compensation of existing employees to new hires.

If we really have similar internal talent making less than this new candidate, the interview team needs to be looking at the comparison of their skills to what the market is paying and consider paying them more. If we do not, the market will, and we will again have to pay another premium to replace them. If you do not make your competitors pay too much to lure your employees away, they will take your people and cause continued challenges regarding cost and production capacity. Pay the new candidate, adjust your existing talent's pay as warranted by their skills and performance, and make the team a more productive place to work. If you allow internal politics and practices to hinder the business decisions you must make, then you are asking the external candidate to carry the burden of that cost. Few will agree to do it. If you then implement a slow decision process, you are going to have a problem in growing your company. If the process extends too long, you will not have to worry about growing the business because your competitors will respond to the market variables faster than you can.

Hiring for Talent – When some leading recruiting companies' are hiring for leadership positions, they find the best two candidates and hire them. It adds bench strength to the organization and builds a future talent pipeline. In growth scenarios, the new employees can accelerate the changes needed as they compete for the position. The work needed will benefit from a couple of viewpoints and will be done more quickly than by one person. If both work out, keep the best one for the position and move the other into another compelling development leadership position. If both do a great job of leading the business, you can also split the business, thus keeping great leaders, and developing leadership talent for future roles.

THINGS TO CONSIDER:

- How much time is your organization spending in discussing or directing the financial and resourcing details of upcoming projects?
- How do you measure the effectiveness of your efforts from the perspective of all stakeholders?
- Are your interview loops and processes in line with the level of the position that you are filling?
- What have you found?

Go to https://winningthewarfortalent.org for more information.

13

LAUNCHING THEIR CAREER WITH YOU

Requisition Preparation > Go to Market > The Search is On! > Assessing Talent > Choosing the Best Candidates > Launching Their Career With You

In our final meeting Jim was in a much better mood. He started the discussion with, "Wow, I am really getting excited about our hiring and the improved results we are going to see. We still have challenges and continue to adjust the process, but we have set up a better model to adjust to those challenges more efficiently. Our first class of hires starts next week so I am super excited about having more resources to do the work we need to do."

Jasmin asked, "Have you contacted the candidates to welcome them, to introduce them to allies and mentors, and to let them know who to go to if they have questions?"

Jim was still very excited. "No, but orientation starts Monday and all of it will work itself out once the candidates begin to figure it all out."

I then added, "I think it is best if we separate 'orientation' from 'onboarding.' Orientation consists of the activities, legal documents, benefits decisions, and access candidates need to begin working with us. Onboarding is the information and resources they need to succeed. Orientation will likely take 45 minutes or so, but onboarding will likely take three to six months. You put all the work into the processes we have discussed in getting the candidates to convert to employees so you will want to protect the investment in making sure they have all the information they need to be successful."

Jim stopped and said, "Wow, it sounds like my leaders still have a lot of work to do!"

To many business leaders, onboarding is another word for orientation. It is not. Orientation refers to providing the information a new employee needs to make decisions about their benefits and some of the logistics associated with the first day (photo ID, access, equipment delivery, tax information documents). There are several acceptable definitions of onboarding, but I consider it to begin when an offer is accepted and continue through the first six months of employment.

Orientation is an important piece of the onboarding process. It is where the company and the hiring team begin to prepare the new employee for success in their new role so they can begin to add value to the company and hiring team as quickly and significantly as possible.

After so much time has been invested, the offer has been extended and accepted, and a great candidate has agreed to join you, it is important to switch your approach a bit. You will want to move from attraction to commitment to the employee's career, which adds maximum value to the company for the expense incurred. We want to get the candidate fully functional as quickly as possible, and ensure the candidate does not change their minds during this time. Most candidates will want to provide a two-week notice to their current company. If they do not hear from the new company during this time, the risk of them going somewhere else increases. During several of my assignments, I have been surprised to see so many hiring managers fully expect recruiting to be the only contact with the candidate. This makes sense, and many recruiters would prefer it, but from a business perspective, the primary contact with the candidate will begin to shift to the business with HR and recruiting support.

In one of my assignments, I studied the orientation process to identify opportunities for improving efficiency. Recruiters were sharing that candidate contact remained high after the offer was extended. Upon review, we realized there were 15 touch points for each candidate from the offer to the first day of work. The candidates were receiving verification mails from all of the departments affected (IT, facilities, ID department, the mailroom, human resources, payroll) independently verifying information, welcoming the new employee, and asking necessary questions to get the candidate started. We decided to dedicate internal resources and external outsourced resources to make the process more friendly to candidates, hiring managers, and key stakeholders within the company to control the flow of communications and reduce duplications. The headcount investment came from the efficiencies we estimated to gain within the recruiter's duties and the process outsourcing costs would be passed to the hiring team at a reasonable rate. Over time, as the recruiters were able to dedicate more of their time to filling more positions, the overall costs of improvement were captured in a reduced cost per hire for the company.

Spending a little time from when candidates accept the offer to when they start can greatly improve their performance in both the short term and the long term. Many of the companies I have worked with in the past have approached orientation in the same way they have always done it. It may be fine in some situations, but with today's technology advancements there are some easy ways to improve the service to the new employee, reducing the questions and confusion manual systems can produce. As we discussed in the story above, if you can do pre-work on some of the more traditional pieces of orientation, you can have a huge advantage over your competition. If this process is great, your candidates will tell their friends, and then whatever employee referral approach that you have decided on can be used to accelerate current and future candidate generation. Some of the components of orientation are as follows:

- Procurement of personalized or departmentalized equipment – Cell phones, computers, headsets, network and information access, and tool access so employees are fully functional with the technology they need to succeed when they walk in on the first day of their new career.
- Procurement of desk accessories – Pens, desk pads, chairs and desk, bulletin board pins, whiteboard markers, stapler, and other information and supplies sitting on their desk in an order they can find and then change if they desire to.
- Any type of marketing materials you want them to have, all with recruiting messages included.
- Directions regarding how to proceed if any of this is missing, or if special requests are to be made.
- Give a tour and links to information about parking, transportation, facilities that are provided, and a general schedule for the first week.
- Introduction to one team member who is there to direct any questions or challenges to the appropriate parties for quick resolution. This "buddy" will also welcome them in the morning, give them the first day schedule, a tour of the facilities, and introduce them to various team members on their team.

If this process becomes automatic and automated, it can really send a message to the candidate about how the organization values them and show them how the company is committed to their success.

One of the best orientations I have personally experienced was with a small, growing technology company. Because they used a partially automated process, all candidates received consistent first day information, including parking garage instructions, train route information, and amenities (food, gym) information with directions on how to activate a badge and gain access. We were supplied with links to benefits so I could pre-register or ask specific questions in person. The orientation meeting took approximately two hours. When new employees showed up for the first day, we knew where to go, who to ask for, and what to expect. When we showed up, they provided the work documentation needed and then an administrative process was conducted while we were in our orientation session. New employees did not have to spend a lot of time on "HR" items during the morning of the first day. The orientation focused on making sure new employees knew who led which initiative and how their role fit into the company business plan. This allowed us to start to envision specifically how we were going to help the business and our career accelerate faster than otherwise planned. The staff was available to answer questions in person for those who needed it, and everyone met the people who were tasked with helping them as employees throughout their career there. I was ready to get started in my new role and was thankful the process was moving quickly. The rest of our time was then shifted to specific guidance on how to succeed, how the company made money, how we contributed to it and how we would be rewarded for it. Individual departments started to get involved in introductions and activities which would help us to make the transition that new employees had agreed to.

In speaking with some companies, they are very proud of their orientation taking two to three days. However, when you speak to the trainers and the corporate staff, it is too much information to digest in those days and that creates confusion and inhibits the learning of new employees. Utilize the efficiencies of automation earlier in the process and use it on this population, resulting in less overall effort and focusing energy on those who are most likely to work with your company. On the first day of work, very little time is then spent on *introducing* orientation processes. Instead, focus on *completion* of the necessary orientation processes.

Onboarding

Onboarding is a much broader and more detailed process that sets the employee up for success in the short and long term. Onboarding should take place within the first six months of employment, until the employee is ready to engage in the long-term programs and initiatives of the company more actively. There are several components top companies include in onboarding, and here are a few:

- **The peer mentor** – The peer mentor is an assigned colleague of the candidate who resides in the organization but outside of the direct team of the new employee. It is an informal way to get other members of the organization to build networks, camaraderie, and teamwork. This person can help the new hire work through all of the small details and issues they will encounter in their first few months of employment. The peer mentor clears the time needed in the first few days for some of the activities to follow and can be available as an informal resource for as long as the participants want. The peer mentor can oversee the results of the orientation, and share feedback and questions with the facilitators so future improvements can be made. They can also assist with the small tactical items or mishaps which may occur. Making introductions, arranging for the introductions to key stakeholders, and general preparation for the first week of work are primary responsibilities for this current employee. This helps them to meet new members and can help them to become people managers and project leaders in the future. They are informal helpers who are not responsible for evaluating the new hire's performance.

- **The manager** – The manager relationship is more formal, is focused on the short- and long-range prospects of the candidate, and is key to ongoing personal performance assessments. Your competition who onboards well will do some of the following activities:

  o **Lunch introductions** – One greatly beneficial thing is to arrange for a manager's lunch with new employees on the first day, followed by a personal performance discussion for the new employee. It is in this meeting that the manager can introduce the performance objectives for the first 30, 60, and 90 days. They would also go over the annual performance metrics for the various parts of the team, including the new employees' roles and those of others they might become interested in in the future.

  o **Team "grab and go" lunch on the second day** – The first lunch is a more personal introduction and is best done off site and free of distraction. The second is held in a central location, is less formal, and allows for team members and key stakeholders to come in and be introduced and visit with the new recruiting team member. It is also a great way for some recruiters to informally visit with stakeholders and model behaviors you feel are important for the new hire. Stakeholders often feel appreciated to be included but can choose not to attend if they do not want to.

o **30-day schedule** – The manager will list all the people they want the new employee to meet with and will assign various team members to assist in coordinating the meetings. This will also include links to any developmental resources, executive presentations, and tutorials, so the new employee knows what to work on when there is down time.

This onboarding is guided by the manager and provides for an accelerated acclimation for the new employee and for a continued acclimation for the rest of the team. It is the manager who can share organization chart details, business goal details, and where the teams they support fit into the rest of the company. The manager also takes the information learned during orientation and applies it to the teams the new employee is going to work with. It is a good example of using the administrative process of recruiting to reinforce the business importance of the team's performance. The other thing it can be used for is to share contact information and encourage ongoing interactions among all team members.

> Do not forget to consider including a few current employees from other departments in some of the onboarding. Some may find it useful and having employees from other departments will add value for the class and for the current employees on their team.

Job Modification in the Short Term

We have spoken about the importance of providing the new employee with the support and comfort which will benefit them as their career progresses. One way to accomplish this is to adjust the tasks of the position so they start small, are tactical, and are important to the learning process. Then, over time, more complex duties can be added. Expecting a new employee to be fully functional is still not realistic, but if you change the stages of what functional means, you can really have a positive impact on the candidate experience and will begin to benefit the team more as more of the work is being handled by the new employee.

> In several of my assignments, the recruiter turnover was high, and the replacement time was long. The group had defined "fully functional" as having a new team member do all the items necessary to operate as a full recruiter. During this time, team resources had to absorb the load of training the new recruiter with no real relief from their own duties. The new recruiter was frustrated, feeling like they were not fully contributing, and the workload of the rest of the team increased as they tried to help to train the new recruiter. It took approximately six months for the recruiter to become fully functional. At one point we were going to have to add more recruiters than we had available to train the new ones.

To rectify this, we broke the recruiting process down into the following components:

- Sourcing for another recruiter
- Scheduling candidates for interviews and managing the associated logistics
- Interacting with managers
- Handling all components of a few requisitions
- Managing the whole process

We were then able to quickly educate the new hire and have them "shadow" peers for an hour or two per day. By the end of week one, they were feeling great because they were submitting candidates for a few roles. The training recruiter was then able to move on to more difficult and strategic tasks. In this model, it was not unusual for the new recruiters to hit their hiring goal within 30 days and to consistently hit every goal by month six. During this time, the training recruiters benefited greatly because the burden of workload was being lifted from the less specialized tasks allowing them to engage in more strategic activities.

It was a tremendous success, not only for the reasons above but because the hiring teams were starting to recognize the changes we had made and were more willing to further contribute to the success of the new recruiters in ways that were under their control.

The main point here is that great companies separate orientation from onboarding and treat both as business processes instead of just administrative ones. New employees can quickly contribute in small ways and then expand their responsibilities in stages. The training employees can then engage at a higher level within their departments, so positive accomplishments are being made at a broader scale in less time than it took previously.

THINGS TO CONSIDER:

- Does your organization differentiate between orientation and onboarding?
- Do your leaders invest the time to train new employees and develop existing employees by expanding their roles as presented here?
- How are you checking this? Do you use surveys to determine the effectiveness of the orientation and onboarding from various stakeholder perspectives?
- For questions and information, does your organization differentiate between orientation and onboarding?
- Do your leaders invest the time to train new employees and develop existing employees by expanding their roles as presented here?
- How are you checking this? Do you use surveys to determine the effectiveness of the orientation and onboarding from various stakeholder perspectives?

Go to https://winningthewarfortalent.org additional information and articles on this topic.

CONCLUSION

As we have mentioned, there is a war for talent. Win it! The recruiting process should be designed with the following guiding principles, and these have been addressed, highlighted, and discussed throughout the text. The priorities of each organization will change based upon their size. Whether it is in a private practice, government agency, or any industry, the candidate population is going to be different, but the basic concepts remain the same.

> **The talent acquisition process is a business process that is business focused with financial implications**

- The talent acquisition process is a business process that is business focused with financial implications – We have discussed the difference between an administrative function and a business practice. And how the ability to execute in the talent acquisition space will have financial and business implications, regardles of the size of the teams involved. Large teams can look at large candidate sets to justify the focus described in this book, but smaller teams are also faced with smaller changes that nevertheless have a larger relative impact on the company.
- The process should be company and candidate focused – By thinking of candidates as potential customers or competitors, it allows your organization to maximize the posi-

tive impact you can have within the talent community. By creating the automated processes which will allow you to provide better service, better outcomes, and quicker response times, you develop a competitive advantage over your competition which is difficult for them to copy.

- Partnership with all involved is required to identify and address challenges with the process as they occur – By removing the view of the interview process as a competition between departments, you can begin to work together to respond to the talent needs of the organization. The ideas and innovations your team creates can then be duplicated in other departments to help the entire organization. All departments will then be benefiting from the candidate generation efforts of the others.

In looking at your organization you will find that some of these activities are already being done well and some are not. Some activities can be added to what you are doing to further improve your performance and can be prioritized based on the degree of impact needed.

Remember: There is a war for talent. Your competition is no longer limited to your industry. Candidates have choices for all positions in many companies at a level which is unprecedented. Companies that best implement the processes presented here will win the war and they will improve the business outcomes of their organization through their talent practices.

Here is how you should begin:

- Look at the chapters and topics of this book.
- Highlight the ones that most apply to you or are already a high priority.
- Use the information and the questions provided to help you to focus on the issues you have identified more clearly.
- Begin to create the solutions which best address the topics you picked.

- There are several topics which will be important to your operation, but remember to include those providing the highest rate of return.
- Once an item is addressed, add another one and continue to monitor each one you add.

As you implement each set of changes, continue to prioritize the remaining tasks, and determine which ones you will address next. By following these steps, your company can begin to improve your financial results. You will also improve candidate and hiring manager satisfaction which will benefit your employees' performance results. All you must do is get started. If I can help to answer questions, share ideas, or present to groups within your company, feel free to contact me at Kevin@Stakelum.com or via https://winningthewarfortalent.org.

REVIEW INQUIRY

Hey, it's Kevin here.

I hope you've enjoyed the book, finding it both useful and fun. I have a favor to ask you.

Would you consider giving it a rating wherever you bought the book? Online book stores are more likely to promote a book when they feel good about its content, and reader reviews are a great barometer for a book's quality.

So please go to the website of wherever you bought the book, search for my name and the book title, and leave a review. If able, perhaps consider adding a picture of you holding the book. That increases the likelihood your review will be accepted!

Many thanks in advance,
Kevin Stakelum

WILL YOU SHARE THE LOVE?

Get this book for a friend, associate, or family member!

If you have found this book valuable and know others who would find it useful, consider buying them a copy as a gift. Special bulk discounts are available if you would like your whole team or organization to benefit from reading this.

Just email Kevin@Stakelum.com or visit www.Stakelum.com.

WOULD YOU LIKE KEVIN STAKELUM TO SPEAK TO YOUR ORGANIZATION?

Book Kevin Now!

Kevin accepts a limited number of speaking/coaching/training engagements each year. To learn how you can bring his message to your organization, email Kevin@Stakelum.com or visit www.Stakelum.com.

ABOUT THE AUTHOR

Kevin Stakelum has led enterprise-level talent acquisition teams for globally ranked corporations and has been engaged in major talent acquisition, development, and management initiatives for over 30 years. He has been officially recognized in the areas of interview automation practices, employment branding, veteran hiring, disability hiring, college hiring, and the hiring of retirees and other specific populations. Kevin has also led initiatives in the areas of internal mobility, diversity leadership organization partnerships, and career development. He has served as an adjunct professor at the University of Louisville in HR management, organizational design, and talent management, for undergraduates and the Experienced MBA programs. He is also the principal/owner of Stakelum Recruiting Consultants located in Louisville, KY.

Kevin holds a Bachelor of Science degree from Louisiana Tech University and a joint Executive Master of Business Administration degree from the University of Kentucky and the University of Louisville.

Kevin can be reached at: www.Stakelum.com

Printed in Great Britain
by Amazon

20147140R00081